Decline of the West?

George F. Kennan
George Urban
Hugh Seton-Watson
Richard Pipes
Michael Novak
Seymour Weiss
Edward N. Luttwak
Eugene V. Rostow
John Lewis Gaddis
Eduard Mark

Edited by
Martin F. Herz

Decline of the West?

George Kennan and His Critics

Ethics and Public Policy Center
Georgetown University
Washington, D.C.

Library of Congress Cataloging in Publication Data:

Decline of the West?

 Includes biographical reference.
 1. World politics—1945- —Addresses, essays,
lectures. 2. Kennan, George Frost, 1904- —Addresses, essays, lectures. 3. United States—Foreign
relations—1945- —Addresses, essays, lectures.
4. Russia—Foreign relations—1945- —Addresses,
essays, lectures. I. Kennan, George Frost, 1904-
II. Herz, Martin Florian, 1917-.
D843.D32 327'.09'045. 78-20038
ISBN 0-89633-018-4

Contents

Foreword

The century of peace preceding World War I can be attributed largely to a global balance of power made possible by the British Navy. Not only did Britannia rule the waves, but she imposed her will on distant peoples. Whatever may be said of British imperial motives or the consequences of British rule in Asia, Africa, and the Middle East, in today's world the old colonial system is morally obsolete.

The United States as the leading Western power after World War II inherited the mantle of British responsibility for maintaining the balance of power. To use current and somewhat more lofty words, we have an obligation to help build a world order that is safe for diversity and peaceful change. But the exercise of this responsibility is more difficult for Washington today than it was for London in the nineteenth century because, among other reasons, we are uncertain of our global role while our chief adversary—the Soviet Union—confidently justifies the use of its power beyond its borders by a theory of revolutionary legitimacy.

Since the mid-1960s we Americans have been debating, if not agonizing over, the proper role of United States power and influence in the vast external realm. The broad consensus that guided our foreign policy from the end of World War II to the middle of the Vietnam War was shattered by weariness with the burden of power, self-doubt about our moral claim to leadership, and diverging views on the nature and seriousness of the threat from the Soviet Union and other Communist states.

Since the fall of Saigon in 1975, we have been trying to establish a new foreign policy consensus—a common understanding of what we as a nation stand for, what our security requires, and what our responsibilities in a dangerous and unpredictable world should be. This difficult task is made more difficult because different people often draw widely differing conclusions from the same events and developments.

Several examples come to mind:

The unwillingness of the U.S. Congress to underwrite funds to support the moderate forces in Angola in 1975 and President Carter's 1977 "commitment" to withdraw American ground troops from Korea are seen by some Americans as signs of vacillation and even retrenchment in the face of Communist pressures. Others see these decisions as prudent measures that properly reflect a new moral and political assessment of U.S. power and interests.

The changing ratio of military power between the United States and the Soviet Union also evokes widely differing interpretations. All Western experts agree that Moscow is forging ahead of Washington in most areas of conventional and nuclear military might. According to the U.S. Arms Control and Disarmament Agency, U.S. military spending from 1967 through 1976 dropped from $120 to $86.7 billion in constant 1975 dollars. During the same period, Soviet military expenditures rose from $79.2 to $121 billion. Thus, in 1976, Moscow was spending almost 40 per cent more for defense than Washington. The ratio has not changed significantly since.

Looking at these same facts, some Americans see an increasing threat to the United States and its allies, while others insist that Soviet designs against the West have moderated or that the United States and its NATO partners already have sufficient strategic and conventional arms to deter or blunt any Soviet assault.

The task of building a new foreign policy consensus is also made more difficult by the confusion of tongues among religious, academic, and political leaders. Many observers at home and abroad have found it difficult to discover a consistent pattern in President Carter's statements on U.S. policy toward friend, foe, and neutral. This was strikingly true of the President's May 22, 1977, Notre Dame University address in which he sought to "connect our actions overseas with our essential character as a nation." Because of its significance, this speech was analyzed in a symposium, *Morality and Foreign Policy,* published by the Ethics and Public Policy Center.

The present collection is a further effort to stimulate reflection and debate on America's role in the never-ending struggle for security with freedom. We do this by presenting and analyzing the evolving views of a distinguished diplomatist and scholar, George F. Kennan. Through four decades of service to his country and through his incisive writing, Mr. Kennan has become a major figure in foreign policy and academic circles. During the past year his utterances have become the center of a swirling controversy on both sides of the Atlantic.

To bring the views of Kennan and his critics to a larger audience in a systematic form, I invited Martin F. Herz, a career U.S. Foreign

Service officer and former ambassador to Bulgaria, to assemble the best recent essays available and to prepare an introduction that would identify the chief points at issue. Ambassador Herz is well qualified for this task. He has served not only in Eastern, Central, and Western Europe, but in the Middle East and Far East as well. He is the author, among other works, of *Beginnings of the Cold War* (1968). Currently he is a Senior Research Fellow at the Ethics and Public Policy Center and Adjunct Professor of Diplomacy at the School of Foreign Service, both of Georgetown University.

ERNEST W. LEFEVER, *Director*
Ethics and Public Policy Center

Washington, D.C.
September 1978

Introduction

In his *Memoirs,* George Kennan recalls his unhappiness with President Truman's March 12, 1947, speech to the Congress in which the President not only recommended American emergency aid to Greece and Turkey, but made certain general statements—which have come to be known as the "Truman Doctrine"—about what the United States should do in similar situations elsewhere. At that time Greece was the victim of a Communist insurgency supported by three neighboring Communist countries (Yugoslavia, Albania, and Bulgaria), and Turkey found itself under pressure from the Soviet Union.

"I believe," President Truman said, "that it must be the policy of the United States to support free peoples who are resisting attempted subjugation by armed minorities or outside pressures. . . . The world is not static, and the status quo is not sacred. But we cannot allow changes in the status quo in violation of the Charter of the United Nations by such methods as coercion, or by such subterfuge as political infiltration. In helping free and independent nations to maintain their freedom, the United States will be giving effect to the principles of the Charter. . . ."

Kennan thought this proclamation altogether too sweeping. He expressed the view—by his own account, even before the President's message—that Truman's pronouncement "placed our aid to Greece in the framework of a universal policy rather than in that of a specific decision addressed to a specific set of circumstances. It implied that what we had decided to do in the case of Greece was something we would be prepared to do in the case of any other country, provided only that it was faced with the threat of 'subjugation by armed minorities or by outside pressure.'"

Nevertheless, Kennan did support what he termed "our limited intervention in Greece" because it met three criteria he stipulated in a lecture to the National War College: 1) The solution to the problem at hand was within our economic, technical, and financial capabilities; 2) The resulting situation, if we did not take such action, might redound decidedly to the advantage of our political adversaries; 3) If we did take the action in question, there was good reason to expect that the favorable consequences would carry far beyond the limits of Greece itself.

The third point is especially interesting because it involves what has later come to be termed, in another context, the "domino effect" (sometimes even dignified with the appellation "domino theory"). Assistance to Greece was justified, first, on strategic grounds: If that country were to be taken over by an externally supported Communist minority, it would have extremely damaging effects on the Western position in the entire Eastern Mediterranean. But the political effects could be even more far-reaching. As Kennan himself pointed out, the United States had to consider the repercussions "in an area even more important from the standpoint of our security: Western Europe."

While these quotations are from the Kennan 1967 *Memoirs,* it should be noted that he was recalling his views of twenty years before, when the Truman Doctrine had been enunciated. Thus, in contemplating what might have happened if we had failed to support Greece, he wrote:

> It was hard to overestimate, in those days of uncertainty and economic difficulty, the cumulative effects of sensational political events. People were influenced, as I pointed out on that occasion to the War College, not just by their desires as to what *should* happen but by their estimates of what *would* happen. People in Western Europe did not, by and large, want Communist control. But this did not mean that they would not trim their sails and even abet its coming if they gained the impression that it was inevitable. This was why the shock of a Communist success in Greece could not be risked.

About three months after the Truman Doctrine speech, Kennan's famous "X" article appeared in *Foreign Affairs* (July 1947). In it he analyzed "the sources of Soviet conduct" and suggested a policy for the West to deal with what he saw as the inherently expansionist character of the Soviet Union. A masterpiece of clarity, the article analyzed the historical and ideological roots of Soviet behavior in international affairs. In a key passage, Kennan wrote:

> The very teachings of Lenin himself require great caution and flexibility in the pursuit of Communist purposes. Again, these precepts are fortified by the lessons of Russian history: of centuries of obscure battles between nomadic forces over the stretches of a vast unfortified plain. Here caution, circumspection, flexibility and deception are the valuable qualities; and their value finds natural appreciation in the Russian or the oriental mind. Thus, the Kremlin has no compunction about retreating in the face of superior force. And being under the compulsion of no timetable, it is a fluid stream

which moves constantly, wherever it is permitted to move, toward a given goal. Its main concern is to make sure that it has filled every nook and cranny available to it in the basin of world power.

These pressures against the free institutions of the Western world, Kennan concluded, "can be contained by the adroit and vigilant application of counterforce at a series of constantly shifting geographical and political points, corresponding to the shifts and maneuvers of Soviet policy, which cannot be charmed or talked out of existence. The Russians look forward to a duel of indefinite duration, and they see that already they have scored great successes." In what has probably become the best-known passage of his closely reasoned article, Kennan wrote:

> This [the relatively weaker position of Russia] would of itself warrant the United States entering with reasonable confidence upon a policy of firm containment, designed to confront the Russians with unalterable counterforce at every point where they show signs of encroaching upon the interests of a peaceful and stable world.

Although Kennan's concept of "containing" Soviet power on a long-term basis was not enunciated publicly until some months after the Truman Doctrine speech, it nevertheless represents the philosophical underpinning of a long period of U.S. foreign policy, including that expressed in the Truman Doctrine. Certainly it was so perceived by the American public as well as by foreign observers of the evolution of American policy.

The concept of containment immediately came under attack from critics of various political persuasions: some, mainly on the right side of the political spectrum, thought it did not go far enough; others, e.g. Walter Lippmann, saw containment as the equivalent of "trench warfare" and thus uncongenial to the American character; and still others, such as former Vice President Henry Wallace, held that keeping the peace could and should be left to the United Nations.

But the most formidable critic of the containment doctrine as it was generally understood was Kennan himself. He described his reactions during the debate on containment, and, when attempts were made later to apply the concept in various parts of the world, in these terms:

> Feeling like one who has inadvertently loosened a large boulder from the top of a cliff and now helplessly witnesses its path of destruction in the valley below, shuddering and wincing at each successive glimpse of disaster, I absorbed the bombardment of press comment that now set in.

In retrospect, he wrote in his 1967 *Memoirs,* he recognized that his article had had serious deficiencies. Since some of those deficiencies were similar to those which he had criticized earlier in the Truman Doctrine, it was not entirely clear why he had not edited or rewritten the *Foreign Affairs* article to convey his thinking more accurately. The first deficiency, he said, had been the failure to discuss the role of Soviet power in Eastern Europe.

The second serious deficiency of the X-Article—perhaps the most serious of all—was the failure to make clear that what I was talking about when I mentioned the containment of Soviet power was not the containment by military means of a military threat, but the political containment of a political threat. Certain of the language used—such as "a long-term, patient but firm and vigilant containment of Russian expansive tendencies" or "the adroit and vigilant application of counterforce at a series of constantly shifting geographical and political points"—was at best ambiguous, and lent itself to misrepresentation in this respect.

The third great deficiency, Kennan continued, had been his failure to distinguish between various geographic areas, and to make clear that the containment of which he had been speaking was not something that could be applied successfully everywhere, or even needed to be done successfully everywhere, in order to serve the purpose he had in mind. Some of these self-criticisms were thus similar to the objections he had voiced about the sweeping language of the Truman Doctrine speech.

Whether by containment or another name, the principle of confronting the Russians "with unalterable counterforce at every point where they show signs of encroaching" was a guiding concept of American foreign policy for at least two decades after the "X" article appeared. The only overt Soviet aggression during that period was directed against countries that tried to liberate themselves from Russian control, and to such situations containment was not applicable; but it seems fair to say that the attack of Communist North Korea against non-Communist South Korea in 1950 would not have taken place if the Soviet Union had not armed North Korea for that purpose and given it the green light. It is significant that Kennan (like many of America's top military and political leaders), having originally recommended against any U.S. effort to defend South Korea against an eventual attack, became aware, when the attack occurred, of the high costs to the United States *elsewhere* if it failed to intervene and to restore the regional balance that had been upset by the Communist attack.

While Kennan disclaimed paternity for the containment doctrine, at least in the form in which it was later applied, his thinking on East-West relations has apparently undergone a significant evolution. His belief that the United States should maintain alliances only with the major democratic industrial powers was already implicit in the exegesis of containment in his *Memoirs;* but he has also come to change his views about the nature of Western society and now even questions whether it is worth defending.

An extreme formulation of the latter thought is found in his letter which first appeared in 1976 in the German newspaper, *Die Zeit* (see selection 1):

> Poor old West: succumbing feebly, day by day, to its own decadence, sliding into debility on the slime of its own self-indulgent permissiveness: its drugs, its crime, its pornography, its pampering of the youth, its addiction to its bodily comforts, its rampant materialism and consumerism—and then trembling before the menace of the wicked Russians, all pictured as supermen, eight feet tall, their internal problems all essentially solved, and with nothing else now to think about except how to bring damage and destruction to Western Europe. . . .

He expresses similar views in other writings. On the danger of Soviet aggression or pressure against neighboring states, he expresses a strong conviction that Western "military enthusiasts" are guilty of confusing intentions and capabilities, making totally unwarranted "worst case" assumptions about the former and congenitally exaggerating the latter.

In his most recent book, *The Cloud of Danger,* published in 1977, Kennan takes positions slightly less extreme than those he expressed in recent articles and interviews in which he seemed to say that it was more important for the West to reform itself than to defend itself. He does recognize the existing fears in Western Europe that our side might be overbalanced in conventional arms by the power of the Soviet Union and its satellites; and, while regarding such fears as irrational ("We have to treat our European friends as a species of psychiatric patient with hallucinations"), he concludes that the American military presence in Europe might have to be increased—to humor the Europeans.

Perhaps the essence of his thinking on military matters is expressed in the passage dealing with intentions and capabilities of the Soviet Union as they are perceived by many Western military experts:

> The assumptions with relation to Soviet strength are as exaggerated as are those that relate to Western European weakness. The belief that stronger

powers dominate weaker ones and dictate terms to them simply by the possession of superior military force, or by demands placed under threat of the use of such force, has extremely slender support in historical experience.

Taken together, these revisions of Kennan's thinking come close to something we used to call "isolationism," though Kennan did himself a disservice in describing his own position as basically isolationist (see selection 2). That he is no longer a believer in "containment" should come as no surprise: he has long parted company with those who believed that approach to be a viable prescription for American foreign policy.

What, then, is his current body of beliefs?

This modest collection seeks to assess to what extent Kennan's current thinking represents a coherent whole, which can be compared with his thinking of thirty years ago. We believe—or at least hope— that the clash of ideas will generate light. The Ethics and Public Policy Center takes no position on the merits of either side of the debate. We believe the reader will be able to grasp the essence of Kennan's current views from the excerpts printed here. We also believe we are giving adequate space to his intellectual adversaries to set forth what they believe to be today's dictates of national security in dealing with Communist states, which have become more numerous and varied since Kennan first wrote about Communism, but which still, in the view of the critics, show tendencies of wishing to "encroach upon the interests of a peaceful and stable world."

From the outset of this project I have enjoyed the support, encouragement, and practical assistance of Dr. Ernest W. Lefever, Director of the Ethics and Public Policy Center. He has himself made some difficult selections, for instance from Kennan's *Cloud of Danger*. Without his advice and guidance this project could not have been brought to fruition.

I also thank Ambassador Kennan for permission to reproduce portions of his book, and express appreciation to him and our other contributors for permission to include their essays from various periodicals which are fully identified at the beginning of each selection.

MARTIN F. HERZ, *Editor*

Washington, D.C.
September 1978

PART ONE

If it is true that there has been a recent evolution in the thinking of Ambassador Kennan, then the early evidence is probably contained in three items of Part One—a letter to a publisher in Germany, an interview with a British political scientist, and a speech which Kennan gave in Washington. These expressions of his views elicit lively controversy. From three directions—historical, moral, political—the critics challenge Kennan's views. Has he perhaps been misunderstood? A more rounded picture of his thinking and a more systematic analysis of it are found in Part Two.

1. Western Decadence and Soviet Moderation

George F. Kennan

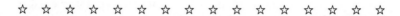

In mid-1976, Die Zeit of Hamburg published a letter from Ambassador Kennan to its publisher, the Countess Marion Doenhoff. The letter, featured as an article or essay, already foreshadowed elements of his controversial November 22, 1977, speech in Washington (see selection 4). In this communication, Mr. Kennan emphasizes the continuity of Soviet policy with its Russian past and criticizes the West for exaggerating the Soviet threat. He also castigates the West for its decadence, self-indulgence, permissiveness, and "rampant materialism." The essay serves as a brief introduction to the debate on both sides of the Atlantic precipitated by Mr. Kennan's views.

Reprinted by permission from *Freedom at Issue*, September-October 1976; the article appeared there under the title "Are All Russians 8 Feet Tall . . . and Is the West Blind to the Threat From Within?"

Meaning of Détente

I AM FREE TO CONFESS that I do not know what détente means. There seems to be an impression about that at some time around 1970 there was a sharp change in U.S.-Soviet relations, marking a new phase in the relationship to be known as détente; that this was based on some sort of an agreement or understanding not only between these two countries but between Moscow and the West generally; but that recently the Soviet leaders have failed to live up to this agreement because they have (a) continued to build up their armaments, (b) intervened, if only indirectly, in Angola, and (c) failed to relax the restrictions on their own citizens. I know of no justification for any part of this belief.

The idea that there was some sort of sharp change in policy and in the relationship between the U.S. and the Soviet Union in the early 1970's was a myth propagated by the Nixon administration for its own internal-political purposes, eagerly supported and inflated by the Western press—or large parts of it, and happily sustained by the Soviet government—once again, for purposes of its own. I don't mean that there were no improvements in the Soviet-Western relationship at the time in question, or that these improvements were not of serious value. But in almost every case, they were changes that were under discussion or in course of preparation well before Mr. Nixon came to office and well before anyone thought of using the term détente in the sense to which we have become accustomed. Circumstances just happened to be favorable, in the early 1970's, to their completion.

Second, there was never any general agreement envisaging a basic change in relations. There were a number of specific agreements, which—so far as I know—the Russians have observed quite faithfully: agreements for academic exchanges, expansion of consular representation, collaboration in the exploration of outer space, etc. Beyond this, there were only the usual cloudy and high-sounding communiqués that follow summit meetings; and there was, of course, Helsinki, about which—a word, presently.

At no time, to my knowledge, did the Russians ever enter into any agreement or understanding of a general nature to halt the development of their armed forces. At no time did they ever encourage us to believe that "détente" would mean the end of their efforts to promote the success of left-wing forces in the Third World; on the contrary, they reminded us a hundred times, if they did so once, that "détente" did not apply in the ideological field. And as for changes in their internal policies: yes, if you want to take seriously the vague generalities of the Helsinki documents; but I must say that it took the wildest naiveté—a naiveté unworthy of serious statesmen or journalists—to suppose that language of this nature, negotiated in the manner in which it *was* negotiated, would really cause the Kremlin to relax the severity of the dictatorship "of the proletariat." For years, I have tried to warn our government against agreements with the Russians involving general language—general terms such as "democratic," "peace-loving," etc.,—and particularly when such agreements are negotiated before the public eye, with the press in attendance; for the Russians tend then to view them as what they call *Demonstrativnye peregovory*—demonstrative negotiations, conducted not for the benefit of the people in the room but through the window, so to speak, for the crowd outside; and in this case, they negotiate in a spirit of *caveat emptor*. I can find no sympathy for statesmen and journalists who so recklessly disregard the lessons of history as to believe that the Helsinki talks were really going to change something important in Soviet behavior.

Expect No Basic Changes

Now, as for what the Russians are doing today: can it not be finally understood and accepted in Western diplomacy that the Soviet relationship to the advanced West is a complicated one, in which there is not much room for maneuver? For many years, ever since the development of the Russo-Chinese conflict in the late 1950's, the Soviet leadership has been driven, in this relationship, by quite contradictory impulses. On the one hand, these men see in the development of their commercial relationship with the West the quickest and most convenient road (not, mark you, the *only* road, merely the quickest and most convenient) to the overcoming of certain of the most painful deficiencies in their own industrial and economic development. Beyond this, they feel a strong need to demonstrate to the Chinese, not just once but constantly and repeatedly, that they are not dependent on their relations with China: that they have other favorable alternatives, that they can live very well, thank you, without China. For this reason, they want the *appearance* of a good and cordial relationship with the West. But they are realists enough to recognize that they cannot have the appearance without having, in some measure, the reality as well; and they

have been willing to make certain compromises along these lines—
compromises which have taken the form of certain of the real Western
gains of the détente period.

On the other hand, these same men are very deeply concerned for
their relations with the remainder of the international communist movement and with the left-wing national-liberation movements of the Third
World—an area in which they are of course being subjected to the
heaviest sort of pressure from the Chinese. For the reasons I have just
cited, they want at least outwardly good relations with the advanced
West; but for reasons of the weightiest sort—reasons having to do both
with their innate distrust of the capitalist world and with their own
image of themselves and of the significance of their own movement—
they would dread a situation in which their security had no other support
than their relations with the West. So they feel compelled to defend
themselves in every way they can against the Chinese charge that they
are not good Marxist-Leninists, that they are selling out the holy faith,
etc. This means that they must continue to talk and to behave, whenever
put to the test, as good, principled Marxist-communists, favoring anti-
European, anti-American and anti-Western movements, encouraging
any political development that even gives the appearance of leading
toward radical-socialist revolution. The West has no right to expect
them to behave otherwise. It has no right to expect them to discourage,
outwardly, a triumph of the Portuguese communists or of the MPLA
in Angola, or what you will. They may hope, secretly, that one or
another of these movements will not succeed (I suspect that this was
the case both with respect to the Portuguese and the Italian communists); but they cannot admit this publicly, for the Chinese would in-
stantly take advantage of it.

The Soviet leaders have attempted to resolve this contradiction by
offering to the Western powers, in effect, relaxation of tensions and
greater collaboration on the *bilateral* plane, while insisting on the right
to behave like a traditional communist power in their relations with
third countries and areas. This, of course, is not ideal, from the standpoint of the West. But it is better than nothing; the gains thus made
represent fairly important improvements over what existed twenty or
thirty years ago; and there is no reason to turn up one's nose at limited
improvements just because one cannot have total ones.

All this has little or nothing to do with the question of military preparations. Here, too, there is a contradiction—or at least the appearance

of one. On the one hand, these Soviet leaders are well aware (much better aware than the Western press seems to be) of the appalling danger represented, not just for themselves but for humanity at large, by the unconscionable quantities of nuclear overkill now in existence, and by the rapid proliferation of the power of disposal over such weapons. They would like to see this danger mitigated; and they are therefore willing, as is evidenced in the SALT talks, to pursue discussions to this end. The fact that they are handicapped in such discussions by their own pathological preoccupation with secrecy does not mean that they would not like to see some positive result flow from them.

Conventional Weapons Increase

At the same time, they remain committed to the development and maintenance of conventional weapons on a scale far greater than anyone else can see the need for. The reasons for this are ones that reach deeply into the Russian past. The maintenance of inordinately large ground forces was a feature of Russian life in the time of Nicholas I, in the time of Alexander III, and in the time of Stalin. Even in the 1920's Russia was maintaining by far the largest ground forces of any European power, although Germany was prostrate, and the French— 2,000 miles away. One must assume that this has to do with a certain inner insecurity; with an awareness of weaknesses assiduously concealed from the outside world; but also with a need to keep large portions of young manpower at all times under disciplined control and available, if need be, for internal use.

I do not mean for a moment to deny that this is a serious problem for the Western powers. On the contrary, I think the West should have made more of an issue of it, in its relations with Russia, than has been the case. But it is not a problem that arose with "détente" or indeed that has anything to do with "détente"; and the fact that it remains unsolved, today, should not be regarded in the West as the result of failure on the Russian part to live up to some general agreements under this heading.

The fact that difficulties continue to exist is no reason for despairing of the whole effort to achieve a better relationship with Russia, and for returning to all the sterile rigors of the Cold War.

Russia is a country ruled today by an old and tired bureaucracy, caught up in the habits and policies and concepts of the past, dimly aware of the inadequacy of all these concepts in the face of the problems of the present, but fearful of change and devoid of constructive ideas. Its leaders, mostly people in their late sixties and early seventies, are not inclined towards major innovations of policy, particularly not risky or adventuresome ones. They face many serious internal problems, and their whole motivation in external relations is basically defensive: defensive against the Chinese political attack, defensive against the disturbing implications of continued Western economic and technological superiority. It is absurd to picture these men as embarked in some new and dark plot to achieve the subjugation of, and the domination over, Western Europe. They are committed, to be sure, to a whole series of habitual postures, reactions, and rhetorical utterances that may appear to bear in that direction. But none of these manifestations of Soviet behavior are new; none are inspired by any belief in the possibility of their early success; and there are none that should be occasioning for Western statesmen any greater anxieties than they were experiencing—say—ten or fifteen years ago before détente ever began to be talked about.

Here, as in the military field, I am not denying that the outlooks and policies and professed purposes of the Soviet leadership do not present serious problems for Western statesmanship—problems which demand their most thoughtful and responsible attention. But I am saying that this is nothing new—that things have been this way for over half a century. And I am saying that Western statesmen will not be aided, in their effort to cope with this problem, by persuading themselves that what they have to contend with is some new and menacing departure in Soviet diplomacy and strategy. They will not be aided by trying to blame the Soviet government for changes in the balance of political forces that are overwhelmingly the consequences of the failures of Western society itself. They will not be aided by first neglecting the development of their own conventional forces and then blaming the Soviet government because the military balance runs in Western Europe's disfavor.

Poor old West: succumbing feebly, day by day, to its own decadence, sliding into debility on the slime of its own self-indulgent permissiveness; its drugs, its crime, its pornography, its pampering of the youth, its addiction to its bodily comforts, its rampant materialism and consumerism—and then trembling before the menace of the wicked Russians, all pictured as supermen, eight feet tall, their internal problems all essentially solved, and with nothing else now to think about except how to bring damage and destruction to Western Europe. This persistent externalization of the sense of danger—this persistent exaggeration of the threat from without and blindness to the threat from within: this is the symptom of some deep failure to come to terms with reality— and with one's self. If Western Europe could bring itself to think a little less about how defenseless it is in the face of the Russians, and a little more about what it is that it has to defend, I would feel more comfortable about its prospects for the future.

2. From Containment to . . . Self-Containment

A Conversation Between George F. Kennan and George Urban

The publication of a thirty-three-page interview with George Kennan in Encounter, *September 1976, drew considerable criticism. In London,* The Times *said: "His pessimism is too facile, too fashionable and perhaps already out of date. . . . Mr. Kennan . . . seems rather more skeptical than is necessary about the continuing validity of his own doctrine of containment." A rejoinder from Hugh Seton-Watson appears in this collection as selection 3.*

The Encounter *interview, conducted by George Urban (co-author of* Detente, *1976, and other books), was published in eleven sections. Of those, we reproduce three because they seem most reflective of the changes that appear to have occurred in Kennan's views: (2) "Can America Continue as a World Super-Power?"; (6) "Cold Warrior or Revisionist Historian?"; and (7) "The Two Disasters."*

Here Kennan, for the first time, describes himself as a qualified "isolationist." Urban observes that Kennan seems to believe that the West, because of its decadence, "doesn't deserve to win," and that it has its priorities wrong. Kennan seems to say: The ecological disaster will be a certain disaster whereas the Soviet threat is contingent—it will probably never materialize, and if it does, we can survive it.

Urban leads Kennan to express other controversial views which are elaborated in Kennan's book, The Cloud of Danger, *from which excerpts appear in Part Two below.*

☆ ☆ ☆ ☆ ☆ ☆ ☆ ☆ ☆ ☆ ☆ ☆ ☆ ☆ ☆ ☆

Reprinted by permission from *Encounter*, September 1976.

Can America Continue
as a World Super-Power?

URBAN: No one is more aware than you that the internal American political process is diffuse, impenetrable and chaotic; and that it is, from such a base, extremely difficult to pursue a consistent and effective foreign policy, especially *vis-à-vis* a power that has a long-term strategy. We have, of course, been aware, at least since Tocqueville, that the political perspectives of democracy are always short-range and therefore debilitating. But this awareness has not helped us very much—rather has it added to our problems.

Since World War II, an unfamiliar responsibility—world leadership—has devolved on American shoulders, but it would seem that neither the American people nor the United States government is willing, or indeed able, to do justice to it in terms of adjusting the American system to its requirements. Can the system be reformed with this end in mind? Is it, on current showing, likely to be so reformed?

KENNAN: I can see no way in which the system can be reformed. I am afraid there is long going to be a tendency for individual legislators and politicians in this country to try to exploit the foreign policy process for their own domestic political ends. As long as they do this, they inflict a sense of incoherence on American foreign policy, because we are pushed into taking actions in the foreign field, not for their effectiveness in the matters with which they purport to deal, but for their ulterior function here at home. It is a self-defeating attitude which reminds me of the tennis player who takes his eyes off the ball because he is too conscious of the problem ''How-am-I-going-to-look-hitting-the-ball?,'' instead of concentrating on what he is doing.

I don't take this to be a great black mark against America, or a sign of the inferiority of American society. If you are going to govern, from a single capital, an area as large and variegated as that which constitutes the United States—everything from Florida to Alaska, and from Northern Maine to Southern California—the only way you can govern without coercion is by a never-ending, elaborate series of compromises between political groups and lobbies; and this method of governing the United States is quite possibly better than the alternatives would be.

But if that is the only way the country can govern itself, then it ought to recognize that this places certain limitations on what it can hope to do in the field of foreign affairs, and that its policy should be a very restrained one.

I do not like the word "isolationism" because it has connotations that are too extreme; but I would say that such a country ought to follow a policy of minding its own business to the extent that it can. When I say I am an "isolationist"—which in a sense I am—I do not advocate that we should suddenly rat on NATO and abandon our West European allies. I don't even mean that we should do anything abruptly to curtail our commitments anywhere. To do so would be a new offence in its own right. But I do feel that we should not accept new commitments, that we should gradually reduce our existing commitments to a minimum even in the Middle East, and get back to a policy of leaving other people alone and expect to be largely left alone by them. We greatly exaggerate the hazards of doing so. Even when people talk, as they now do, about the consequences of Soviet interference in Angola, the dangers of what is really involved in Angola for the United States are egregiously exaggerated. It may be there are dangers for the *Angolans*; but for us the dangers are not significant.

URBAN: Don't you think this kind of attitude would leave the world wide open to Soviet territorial and political expansionism? Wouldn't it, above all, deliver Western Europe to the Soviet Union?

KENNAN: We should not cut our commitments to Western Europe abruptly. But Western Europe has, since the War, leaned on us more heavily than is good for Western Europe itself. We have been a form of escape for our European allies. They have seen us as saving them the necessity of having a policy either towards Eastern Europe or Germany, which is, of course, very agreeable to them; but it must now end. A gradual American withdrawal, and a gradual assumption of much greater responsibilities by the West Europeans for what is, after all, principally their own defence and political future would be all to the good.

URBAN: You don't think a "Finlandisation" of Western Europe would eventually result from granting the Soviet Union what it would probably interpret as an unlimited right to prospect the world for influence?

KENNAN: The comparison that has been drawn between Finland's position *vis-à-vis* the Soviet Union and that of Western Europe is neither fair to the Finns—whose position is not all that weak or humiliating (they have materially *increased* their freedom of action in the last 25 years)—nor is it fair to Western Europe, because the latter's relationship to Moscow rests on wholly different geopolitical, demographic and economic realities than that of Finland. There is, for example, no reason that I can see why Western Europe should not put up a respectable conventional force of its own. In terms of population and industrial potential, Western Europe is at least fully equal to the Soviets. That it hasn't the military muscle which it ought to have is entirely due to a lack of political will. Western Europe is far too addicted to its material comforts, and values prosperity far too highly, to make the necessary sacrifices. But if that is so, "Finlandisation," if it ever comes, will be a self-inflicted wound.

You talk about the defence of Western Europe—I am wondering whether "defence" is the right word, and whether the greatest danger to Western Europe is not within itself, for the general decadence of Western European society is one of the most tangible realities that hits even a fleeting visitor. I won't go into details, but let me just mention a random sample of ominous developments such as the inability of Britain to improve its industrial productivity which is, incredibly, less than half of that of Germany, and to put the British trade union system on a modern footing. I am equally amazed by the inability of Denmark and Holland to put an end to the pornographic invasion that has overcome them. This betrays a terrible lack of self-confidence and a total confusion of values. The same thing is true of the German student disorders which still remain a serious matter in a number of universities. And what is one to think of the failure of the Berlin Senate to prevent the destruction of the Free University? The challenges are brutal and ubiquitous—the responses pitifully feeble or non-existent. Western Europe has lost a sense of the fitness of things, and that *is* the meaning of decadence.

I sometimes wonder what use there is in trying to protect the Western world against fancied external threats when the signs of disintegration within are so striking. Wouldn't we be better advised if we put our main effort into making ourselves worth protecting?

A couple of years ago, in the course of our usual summer cruise in the Baltic, my family and I put in at a small Danish port which was having a youth festival. The place was swarming with hippies—motorbikes, girl-friends, drugs, pornography, drunkenness, noise—it was all there. I looked at this mob and thought how one company of robust

Russian infantry would drive it out of town.

Now many of these fellows would change their spots and prove very valiant people indeed if you appealed to them and presented to them a cause they thought was worth defending. But many of them would not be able to—many of them are too run-down by drugs and the other effects of a permissive physical life.

URBAN: Calls for social and, really, spiritual regeneration are never absent from your writings; and, personally, I find them difficult not to go along with. But such calls, while fully justified, tend to divert our attention from what we have to do right now in an unregenerate and ugly world, but the only world we have. Will Soviet power wait for our moral renewal?

KENNAN: The Russians are not in a good position to take advantage of our great weaknesses today. They have troubles of their own, enough to keep their attention riveted on other things (I need not rehearse what they are). So I don't think they will capitalise in the near future on the disturbing state of Western Europe. But let me remind you that Western Europe's troubles are not only of a moral and cultural character. One has also to take into account the state of Italy which is almost incapable of governing itself; the disarray and uncertainty all over the Iberian Peninsula; the conflict between Greeks and Turks; and the approaching crisis in Yugoslavia with Tito's death. In the face of all these predicaments affecting the non-Soviet part of Europe, I wonder whether there isn't a certain misplacement of emphasis on the external dangers which are said to be threatening Western Europe.

URBAN: The net effect of what you are saying is: the United States is congenitally incapable of performing a consistently sustained world role; Western Europe, which is decadent and sunk in self-seeking materialism, is hardly worth defending. In any case, the external dangers are (you argue) probably imaginary, whereas the internal ones are real.

But let me assume two things. First, that the Soviet leaders mean what they say when they tell us that they have every intention to exploit the crises of Western society and to support, wherever they can, wars of "national liberation." Secondly, that Western society will, in the short run, not change significantly enough to introduce a fundamentally new element into the East-West relationship. If all this is true, doesn't your attitude amount to a kind of political quietism which would, in effect, mean handing a world hunting-license to the Soviet Union?

KENNAN: I don't believe it does. The ideological approach of the Soviet Union is at least 70-80 years out of date and has very small appeal anywhere. Portugal has furnished an important lesson: it has shown that we have come a long way since 1917—we are not going to have a repetition of the October Revolution, we are not going to have a Bolshevik seizure of power in any of the West European countries. The extraordinary resistance put up by the Portuguese Socialists shows that even in a country as poor as Portugal and as lacking in democratic tradition, a totalitarian takeover can be, and was, effectively resisted.

It seems to me that the future of Western Europe lies along moderate socialism, and this socialisation of Western Europe harbours dangers for the Soviet Union: the example of the West European nations opting for a generally socialist line of development and detaching themselves from the United States will put great strain on the Soviet hold over Eastern Europe. The East European governments, particularly those straining for greater freedom from Soviet control, are going to say: "Why must *we* submit to this? Europe is no longer in a state of militant confrontation. Most of Western Europe is socialist. The United States is no longer there as a great imperialistic power. There is no more justification for the Soviet control of half of Europe. . . ." The disarray in Western Europe is bound to unleash disarray in Eastern Europe; it cuts both ways.

URBAN: It may or it may not. American power, or NATO power, has not been able to stop the rot in Western Europe, whereas Soviet power has, brutally and repeatedly, stopped this disintegration of Eastern Europe and is, under the banner of proletarian internationalism, or some other slogan, certain to do so again, no matter how "socialist" Western Europe may become. In any case a significant loosening-up of Moscow's control of Eastern Europe does not at all appear to be an American priority.

But to come back to your point: what you are implying is that the age of faith has come to an end both in the East and the West—on our side, a profound scepticism has destroyed our adherence to formal religions and undermined our trust in the values, tastes and sensibilities of what has traditionally been regarded as European culture. In the East, the appeal of Communism as an ideology is utterly exhausted. We are, then, talking of the clash of two secularisms, each groping for a new guiding principle.

KENNAN: We are talking about the disintegration of both militant faiths and strong ideological beliefs; but we are also talking about the disintegration of the old forms of great-power imperialism. I don't believe in the ability of the Russians to control Western Europe. They just would not know how. They are too crude and clumsy for any such exploits. Such indeed is their lack of sophistication that they have great difficulty in controlling even those parts of Europe which are under their hegemony.

By the same token, I don't believe in the ability of the United States to control any great part of the world. When people speak today of the Russians "getting" Angola, I don't know what they mean, any more than what they meant when they talked of our "losing" China. Nobody but the Angolans will make anything out of Angola—least of all the Russians with their multiple handicaps, especially in an African setting. No one can seriously believe that Angola will be turned into a Soviet republic on the Uzbekistan model. With the exception of Eritrea, the Russians have had nothing but serious reversals in their African policies. So it is up to us to grasp the nettle and tell the world that we are willing to leave such territories alone. We should come out firmly and frankly in the United Nations and say: "We are prepared to have nothing to do with this area. There will not be one penny of American money, not a single American rifle sent to Africa. The CIA will leave it totally alone on the assumption that the Soviet Union will do likewise. . . ." I think we could, with such a policy, put great pressure, through African opinion, on the Soviet leaders.

URBAN: I find your trust in the power of example most appealing, for it assumes the basic goodness and rationality of man; but I wonder whether there is room for this kind of sentiment in the hard world of international competition. Can you see professional revolutionaries of the stamp of Stalin, or Lenin, or even of the present conservative but expansionist hierarchy, being swayed by this kind of consideration? Their reaction would not be that the Americans have shown a noble example which they (the Russians) must follow, but rather that American capitalism has become so weak-kneed that they may safely push ahead wherever opportunity beckons.

I do, of course, realise that the idea of setting the world an example by our Western works rather than power, and the related notion of passive resistance, are basic to your approach to international affairs.

They were there in your 1957 BBC Reith Lectures, where you said that in the event of a Soviet-American disengagement, European defence should be based on paramilitary forces on the Swiss territorial model:

> The training of such forces ought to be such as to prepare them not only to offer whatever overt resistance might be possible to a foreign invader but also to constitute the core of a civil resistance movement on any territory . . . overrun by the enemy. . . .

And on nuclear competition you said:

> Let us divest ourselves of this weapon altogether; let us stake our safety on God's grace and our own good consciences and on that measure of common sense and humanity which even our adversaries possess; but let us at least walk like men, with heads up, so long as we are permitted to walk at all.

Am I right in detecting a puritanical sense of guilt in all this—a feeling that America is too rich, too powerful, too vulgar, too brash, and *eo ipso*: guilty? Guilty, above all, because it has not suffered where others have suffered, and has yet to be brought low . . .?

KENNAN: Possibly, possibly. My main reason for advocating a gradual and qualified withdrawal from far-flung foreign involvements is that we have nothing to teach the world. We have to confess that we have not got the answers to the problems of human society in the modern age. Moreover, every society has specific qualities of its own that we in America do not understand very well; therefore I don't want to see us put in a position of taking responsibility for the affairs of people we do not comprehend. I would like to see us influence the world, if we can, by the power of our example to the extent that other people wish to follow it and find it applicable to themselves. But I have, as you know, always very emphatically rejected the concept of the universality of the American experience. Our national experience was never shared by any country and will never be shared by any country in the future. Never again will it be given to a national society to develop a vast, unpopulated area in the northern, temperate zone of the world. Think of the potential wealth of this continent, and the way in which people harnessed it to their needs, and also devastated, by their greed, its lakes and forests and sea-boards. All this wealth and space presented possibilities in America which have made the American outlook unique, and therefore inapplicable to any other society.

URBAN: It has fallen to the United States to lead the world, but the

United States can offer no leadership. Isn't this, too, an almost unique fact in history?

KENNAN: Leadership cannot be given for the two reasons we have already mentioned: *(1)* because the United States has nothing much to say to the outside world, and *(2)* because the kind of government we have does not permit, even if we *had* a valid message to impart, the shaping of that message into a consistently pursued foreign policy.

I had the experience some years ago of making a call on one of the African leaders who shall be nameless. The meeting was arranged by some of my friends—I wasn't myself very anxious that it should take place.

"I appreciate your receiving me," I said to this African leader, "but I am embarrassed; my friends asked me to call on you, yet I have nothing to say to you and I don't think my country should either."

"What do you mean by that?" he asked.

"I hesitate to say anything, partly because I think we have no answer to your problem, and partly because I feel anything said would be misinterpreted—that is the atmosphere growing up around us." However, he pressed me to say something. "What do you think the United States ought to do with regard to us?," I was asked.

"Leave you absolutely and strictly alone," I said. "If I had anything to do with it, you would have no cause to complain that the United States took any interest in you except at your own insistent request. Other than that we would leave you absolutely in peace."

He threw back his head and laughed: "You can't do that—you are caught here—you can't opt out."

But I don't think we are necessarily caught in Africa, or anywhere else for that matter. We should, for a start, proceed roughly like this: if people from the developing world came to us with requests saying "We want this or that from you by way of help or advice," I would first ask them: "Why do you think we ought to give these things?" And if we did give them, I would say: "We want it to be firmly documented that these things were given at your request, your initiative, not ours." This would prevent a great many misunderstandings about American neo-colonialism, imperialism, etc. Incidentally, this is the way we ought to have behaved to De Gaulle in the years of his power.

URBAN: I am not sure that your African leader's cry, "You are caught," is all that far-fetched. Raymond Aron remarks in his recent book 'on the American reluctance to bear the burdens of hegemony: "One cannot help wondering at times whether the American republic will ever attain maturity and whether it will at length realise that power implies rights and duties—limited rights and permanent duties."

In a sense I am more worried about your insistence that the United States has nothing to say to the world than by the nature of the American system which, as you say, inhibits the United States from putting across whatever it may have to say to the world. After all, the latter *may* be open to reform, whereas the evaporation of American self-confidence is probably beyond repair in the foreseeable future.

What I have more particularly in mind is something you have, I know, always roundly condemned: the idealistic, moralising streak in the American self-image and American foreign policy. While, in 1976, this may strike one as arrogant or unsophisticated, it has, in the past 150 years, certainly been one of the great assets of American foreign policy. The examples one could cite to support this assertion are so numerous, especially from Czarist Russia and Eastern and Southern Europe, where the promise of America was most widely appreciated, that I shall simply state the fact, wondering whether, if your policy of what one might call American "self-containment" were here to stay, the United States would not be depriving itself of its entire historic magnetism.

KENNAN: If the idealistic component in American policy *has* ever been a force in its own right, it has been confused and really nullified by the crimes and mistakes of recent years: by Viet Nam, by the stupidities of the CIA, by the violation of the democratic process as witnessed by Watergate, and so forth. It would take a long period of withdrawal, a quiet time of minding our own business and rethinking our national purpose, to persuade the world that we had, *if* we had, anything worth while to say to it.

Cold Warrior or
Revisionist Historian?

URBAN: You have not quite satisfied my curiosity whether the symbiosis in your writings of the "Cold Warrior" and the "revisionist" historian (and I am using both labels, *faute de mieux*, with great reluctance) is sufficiently explained by a kind of sublimated gut-reaction on your part to the conventional wisdom of authority. I have mentioned, by way of an example, the incongruity which exists between your "long telegram" in the winter of 1946, and your 1952 despatch "The Soviet Union and the Atlantic Pact." Clearly, you did not suffer fools gladly, especially those set above you in the hierarchy; and I think it is fair to say that you were, by temperament, a "resigner." Do these factors tell us the whole story?

KENNAN: No, they don't. I would not want you to think that the incongruity which you notice stems from some perverse obstructionism, or one-upmanship, on my part. Let me explain what the incongruity was about, and why each of the two, seemingly irreconcilable, strands of my argument was entirely justified in the context in which it was put forward.

Under the Roosevelt administration, both before the War and during the War, there was a wide measure—and for many of us who were serving in Moscow, a disturbing measure—of naïvety and shallowness in the judgments of our governmental leaders with regard to the Soviet Union. This, we felt, was a danger of great seriousness which we had to combat. Soviet-American relations could not be dealt with by those easy and really childish methods which commended themselves to FDR; that is to say, by one-sided American gestures which were expected to appeal to the Soviet leaders, and especially Stalin, personally. (I was shocked to discover that Roosevelt had at one point invited Stalin to involve himself in American domestic politics by sending Stalin a private request to dissuade the United States Communist Party from supporting him at the presidential election lest this support should prove embarrassing to him.)

In the immediate post-War period, when I wrote my "long telegram," I was especially concerned to bring our people in Washington to understand that, before they could effectively deal with the Soviet leadership about the future of Europe or anything else, they would have to prove to it that we would not allow Moscow to win by methods of infiltration and concealed aggression—that the West had sufficient virility, sufficient firmness, and sufficient self-confidence to prevent itself being undone by those means. In the latter part of the War we had led Stalin to believe that Western Europe was being reduced to so pathetic a state in terms of military and economic power and self-confidence, and that the United States was motivated by such a sweeping naïvety with regard to Soviet power, that without any further military action at all, the Soviet Union could soon eliminate the United States from the whole Eurasian landmass and pretty much have it its own way throughout the world. It was clear to me that, so long as the Russians entertained such ideas, we had no hope of dealing with them effectively. Therefore, in 1945 and 1946, I urged Washington to stiffen up and disabuse Moscow of these illusions because I was convinced (and I said so in my despatches) that only when we had proven to the Russians that they could not get what they wanted without dealing with us, would they consent to deal with us.

The effort to enlighten the United States was almost more successful than I had supposed. (I do not, of course, credit myself personally with that success because American opinion was in the process of undergoing a profound change which had deeper reasons.) By the winter of 1947–48 the success of the exercise was amply demonstrated, and the psychological triumph of the Marshall Plan clinched that demonstration. It was my expectation—and I believe I can speak here for my late colleague, Chip Bohlen—that once we arrived at that point, we would sit down with the Soviet leaders and talk to them about the future of Europe in order to see whether we couldn't get some agreement on a general withdrawal of their power and our power, but on terms which would make it possible for the rest of Europe to live.

At that point I found that I had, so to speak, oversold my bill of goods, that our people had become so persuaded of the hostility of the Soviet leaders that they would now wholly dismiss the idea of ever dealing with them about anything. We had many people here, of whom John Foster Dulles was one, who felt that the only way in which we could ever make headway against Moscow was to develop enormous military strength and get the Soviets to do what we wanted them to do by putting them under threats and pressure. And I am fairly sure that the nuclear weapon, the possibilities and impossibilities of which everyone misunderstood except Stalin, encouraged this line of thinking. Washington was obsessed by the idea that the Cold War had to be thought of in exclusively military terms.

I was appalled by all this. I saw no hope in it, and I did not believe that we should take part in any effort to overthrow the Soviet régime. First, I did not think such an attempt would be successful; and, second, even if it were successful, I did not think we had an alternative to offer. In case of a full-scale war, complete victory was all but impossible, whether nuclear weapons did or did not exist. I was shocked by the simplicity of thought which was overtaking people in this country: they were putting Stalin into the image of Hitler, thinking that the Soviet threat was the same kind of thing the Nazi threat had been. Of course, it wasn't at all, and I don't think I need go into arguing why. We were in the middle of the Cold War. My whole thought (to repeat a point I want to stress) in pleading initially for a firm Western stance was to enable us eventually to talk to the Russians so effectively that we could get them to withdraw from the centre of Europe, for the Soviet presence there seemed to me catastrophic for the present and future of the entire continent. Well, I discovered to my horror (and I had the same experience with my Reith Lectures in 1957) that very few people in the Western world wanted to have the division of Europe removed. Most Western Europeans were still more afraid of Germany than they were of Russia, so that the division of Germany, with the United States holding the fort with its troops in Germany, suited them rather well.

This again was something I had to oppose—I never believed that the present division of Europe could be a lasting arrangement, and I stated my reasons for saying why it could not in my Reith Lectures; and even today, I can find very little to fault in them. One reason was the impossible situation of Berlin. But there was also a deeper reason, which few have consented to recognise down to this day: even if we do accept the division of Europe (as apparently we do) with very little concern, we cannot be sure that it will be at all times acceptable to the people of Eastern Europe. We have already had two extremely serious warnings, in the Hungarian revolution and the 1968 Czechoslovak events, to mention only two of the major upheavals—and, you know, one isn't often given more than two warnings in life. What are we going to do the next time there is trouble? What is our policy going to be if one of the East European countries does manage to free itself from Soviet tutelage? As things are, we won't have any policy for it—we won't have any place for it. To take it into NATO would be to make a military demonstration against Moscow, which Moscow can't accept.

URBAN: After your Reith Lectures, Raymond Aron said in a famous symposium that Europe could put up with an absurd or even with an unjust situation, but it could not put up with an ambiguous situation. As (Aron said) the division of Europe was absolutely clear-cut and the absurdities were well respected, the division was acceptable. This is a stance which ignores the restiveness of the East European nations and tacitly assumes that if restiveness were to lead to renewed trouble, the Soviet divisions would act as they always have done, and the West would remain as inactive as it always has been.

I notice that Dr. Kissinger, speaking with the voice of Helmut Sonnenfeldt, appears to have more complex thoughts about the division of Europe. He does recognise that the strained relationship between the peoples of Eastern Europe and Moscow is a great source of instability in Europe, and a greater danger to world peace than the conflict between East and West. He notes that the Kremlin has not been able to acquire any "organic" sense of loyalty in Eastern Europe, and that it relies, therefore, on the presence of sheer military power. He cautions against any excessive zeal on the part of the United States to jeopardise the chances of a more organic relationship between the East European nations and Russia; and he expresses the hope that East European aspirations for greater autonomy, which he supports, will be contained within the Soviet geopolitical context.

You have just asked: how would the West react if some of the East European countries tried to liberate themselves from Russian hegemony? What is the political context in which you would visualise such a liberation?

KENNAN: Look at what has already happened in Eastern Europe. The Yugoslavs have liberated themselves. The Finns, to whose plight the West Europeans love to compare themselves when they talk of "Finlandisation," have, if anything, moved from a restricted sense of sovereignty to a much fuller sense of sovereignty, rather than the other way round. At one time the Minister of the Interior was a Communist, and the police were also under Communist control; but that is no longer so. Today the Finns enjoy complete freedom in their internal affairs. Look at what the Rumanians have accomplished. They follow in many ways, though not in all ways, a highly independent line. Or take Hungary, where the 1956 revolution, although ostensibly a failure, actually changed the internal situation materially for the better, so much so that in a curious way Hungary is leading a substantially independent existence under the Communist dispensation.

All these features are producing a state of affairs in Eastern Europe which is very different from what we saw there in the late 1940s and 1950s. Not only that, but we don't know what the future may bring. We don't know what sort of an impact the forthcoming change in the Soviet leadership is going to have on the sensitive texture of East

European politics. Of course, nothing at all may happen. The party may hold together, younger men may be brought in without friction or upheavals, and so on. But, on the other hand, the dénouement may be quite different. Things may occur which will suddenly confront Western Europe and the United States with the need to have something it has never had since before World War I, that is, a policy towards Eastern Europe, and a viable policy at that.

But these are not my only reasons for opposing the division of Europe. It is to me a tragedy that half of Europe is now constrained to live under a different intellectual and cultural discipline than the other half.

URBAN: So long as the system is not frontally provoked, Moscow's tactical permissiveness in Eastern Europe can go quite far. But as soon as it is thought that the system itself is challenged, Moscow clamps down with great severity. We saw this in 1956 and 1968. Today, the Rumanians have a certain licence because their dissent is limited to foreign policy. Internally they do not challenge the legitimacy of the Soviet model of society; in fact, they are taking trouble to endorse it. Hungary seems to be a borderline case. There, under protestations of external and internal orthodoxy, a good deal of economic and cultural liberalism is tolerated. But one would probably do well to think of it as no more than a court-jester's licence which stands to be revoked the moment it ceases to be a convenient way of relieving tension and begins to impinge on the system. (Whether, of course, the licence *could* be revoked is another matter.)

KENNAN: One thing that has been widely missed by people in judging events in Eastern Europe is the Russians' willingness to put up with a great deal in terms of internal change in these countries, even in a direction they might not approve of, provided it is done with a hammer from the top and without any suspicion of spontaneity from below. What they cannot tolerate, and I suppose this was one of the key elements in the Czechoslovak situation in 1968, is any form of spontaneous reform. They will, for example, permit the East Germans to put into effect economic reforms much more far-reaching than those which were envisaged by Dubcek, as long as it is done dictatorially—as long as the Party is seen to be fully in control.

URBAN: There is also the reluctance to see the client states acquire certain liberties and living standards which the Russians themselves cannot afford to have. If so, isn't Eastern Europe up against an immovable object? Won't East Germans, Poles, Czechs, and Hungarians, by virtue of their cultural seniority, always demand certain things which the Russians will not demand, much less achieve?

KENNAN: The whole concept of Soviet hegemony over Eastern Europe is unsound even from the Russian point of view. Moreover, the prospects of a continuing Soviet hegemony there are undermined by the gradual loss of Soviet leadership of the world communist movement: as the large West European Communist parties become independent from Moscow, the East European parties will have alternative poles of orientation. This could be very important.

For example, I am persuaded that the Yugoslav defection had a great deal to do with the fact that the Rumanians broke ranks on certain important aspects of Soviet foreign policy. Now if—and it appears not impossible—the Italian Communists came into a position of power, this would affect the parties in Eastern Europe even more forcefully. Given an ideological alternative, the East European Communists could claim a degree of freedom from Moscow without suggesting that they were "going over to the capitalists." They could argue: "We find this or that commendable in Chinese, or Italian, or French Communist ideas which we think we ought to be able to adopt. We are not departing from Marxism, and we are not joining the enemy. . . ."

Let me say a word at this juncture about the intellectual background of the growing respectability of West European Communism. Take the French Communist Party. For a number of years it has been a party of protest, and it has occupied that part of the spectrum in French politics which is normally occupied by a strong movement of protest. But if you look at French politics as a whole, I am struck there too (as I am when I look at other parts of Europe) by the sweeping power of Marxist ideas among the student youth and intellectuals. Even a newspaper like *Le Monde*—one of the world's best papers—is now profoundly socialistic in spirit, and not just moderately socialistic, because whenever there is an issue between Peking or Moscow and the West, it instinctively supports the Communist side. I find this quite appalling.

URBAN: Doesn't this show that intellectuals are no better, even if they are perhaps no worse, than other mortals? That they are desperately in need of a small number of simple certainties. . .

KENNAN: . . . And they reach for the false ones if they cannot find genuine certainties.

URBAN: Marxism may be old-fashioned and irrelevant, but it has the soothing aura of faith, and that is what most intellectuals, and indeed most people, are really after. I suppose we are at heart all children grasping for father-images, and the worse the chaos around us, the simpler the images that attract us. That the decadence of our civilisation should coincide with the infantilism of our political culture—doesn't this have an awesome appropriateness about it?

KENNAN: I *can* explain the phenomenon, and yet I cannot really understand it. The naïvety of Marxism-Leninism, and its irrelevance to contemporary conditions, have been so *amply* demonstrated at every turn! And yet, here you have a great section of German, and French, and Italian student youth violently exercised in its favour. Of course, there may be reasons for desiring a greater measure of *dirigisme* in public affairs in the Western countries; I want it myself for ecological reasons rather than social ones—so that may have something to do with it.

But I am still amazed at the shallowness of understanding that animates even people in *Le Monde,* and the double standards they so liberally apply. Any régime that chooses to call itself Marxist can be sure that its brutalities and oppression will be forgiven, whereas any régime that does not is stamped as being of the Right, in which case the slightest invasion of the rights or liberties of the individual on *its* territory at once becomes the object of intense indignation.

It is a minor blessing that, after Hungary and Czechoslovakia, Moscow has never recovered its prestige in the eyes of the West European Communists and thus ceased to be the automatic beneficiary of the radicalism of the West European student youth. In fact, there has been a tendency for latter-day Western Communists to associate themselves much more with anti-Western, nationalist, left-wing movements of the Third World than with Moscow. Apparently the criterion of their affections is the degree of hatred of a given external movement for the West, and especially for their own societies. I asked a Norwegian student recently what it was that the radical students at the University of Oslo most admired—what did they look up to as an example of a hopeful civilisation? After considerable brooding and thought-taking, he said it was . . . Albania!

Can one think of anything more miserable than the régime in Albania? Obviously there is not one shred of reality in this view—no interest at all in the objective truth about Albania. Albania is picked up simply because it seems to be a club with a particularly sharp nail at the end of it with which to beat one's own society, one's own traditions, one's own parents. This is a rebellion against Western Europe—it is not one in favour of anything much else.

The Two Disasters

URBAN: To come back to the division of Europe: you were saying that the Finns have come to enjoy complete domestic independence. My recent visit to Finland leaves me wondering whether this is really so. The Finns have imposed on themselves, either under thinly-veiled pressure or the threat of pressure, certain self-denying ordinances of which self-censorship of the press is one—and perhaps the most harmful as well as the most spectacular.

KENNAN: The Finns have put certain restraints on themselves in matters which they felt would give serious offence on the other side of the border. But Finland is a small country of 4 million people which has a long and extremely exposed border with the Soviet Union and lies very close to Russia's second city. I cannot see how that can be compared to the position of Western Europe. I have said earlier, but let me repeat it, that Western Europe has a larger and infinitely more sophisticated as well as industrially more advanced population than the Soviet Union. Its industrial potential is much greater than that of the Soviet Union, and it is separated from the Soviet Union by a band of buffer states. Clearly, the analogy with Finland is totally inapplicable.

Now this brings me back to a point where my own thinking parts company with that of the whole of the West European community, namely the question of nuclear blackmail and political/military pressure.

Stalin said: the nuclear weapon is something with which you frighten people with weak nerves. He could not have been more right. No one in his right senses would yield to any such thing as nuclear blackmail. In the first place, it would be most unlikely (as is the case with most forms of blackmail) that the threat would be made good if one defied it. Secondly, there would be no point in yielding to it. Any régime that has not taken leave of its senses would reject the nuclear threat. "Why in the world should we give in to this?" it would argue. "If we do what you want us to do today in the name of this threat what are you going to ask us to do tomorrow? There is no end to this process. If what you want us to do is to part with our independence—you will have to find others to do your work for you, and that means that you will have to take ultimate responsibility for running this country. We are not going to be the people to turn this government into an instrument of your power. . . ."

We had experience of this kind of situation during the War with the question of the Azores. I was myself deeply involved in it, and it was quite clear that if we came along and threatened (as we almost did) Salazar and said: "You give us these bases or else we will take them," he would have picked up his hat and said: "If I have brought my country to a pass where I have to deal under this type of pressure, I am obviously not a fit ruler of this country. You will have to find someone else for it."

No one would give in to this kind of pressure; nor does anybody use this kind of blackmail. Great governments do not behave that way. Of course, Hitler did with Hacha, in the case of Czechoslovakia; but Hitler was an exception, and I am not sure that Hacha and the Czechs were wise to yield to this anyway.

URBAN: Nevertheless, the United States government got the Azores bases, and Salazar did not resign. The American threat was sugared by Roosevelt's letter of guarantee that after the War the bases would be returned; and this was, as we know, the result of your personal intervention with the President and Harry Hopkins. But I would find it difficult to accept that Salazar was not acting in the knowledge of American power, or that any Portuguese government could have ultimately resisted that power.

KENNAN: Roosevelt's guarantee entirely changed the nature of the American approach. Far from acting under a threat, the Portuguese permitted (in addition to the military facilities we requested) Pan American to construct a second airport on the Azores—on behalf of the Portuguese government. This, then, was a transaction between independent governments.

But to resume my argument: when we come to the question of conflict between the Great Powers, there is no nuclear war that could be other than catastrophic for all countries indulging in it; and I think the Russians are well aware of this. The last thing in the world they are going to do is to threaten other governments by saying: "You do what we want you to do or else we'll drop nuclear bombs on you." This is childish; no great government behaves in that way, and the Russians are not going to.

It is of the most profound importance that the proliferation of nuclear weapons be halted. These weapons, which are much too terrible to be in human hands—ours or anybody else's—must be eliminated from the spectrum of possible military instruments. I am deeply distressed that the United States government takes no helpful action along these lines. We could be much bolder, not so much in the negotiations, as in our unilateral policies. The nuclear weapon is simply not a rational means of political pressure or action. It is top-heavy and cannot be used for gaining political advantage except against people who, as Stalin said, have weak nerves.

URBAN: Are you advocating unilateral nuclear disarmament?

KENNAN: Not all at once, or not without reciprocation, but if no one takes the lead in imposing self-restraint in the development of these weapons, we are never going to get any reduction of them by negotiation.

URBAN: You are a man of great goodwill and, at heart, an optimist, though a pessimistic optimist. You first talk of "great governments" which will not commit certain crimes because of some unspoken *noblesse oblige* principle which is implied in your use of the word "great." Now you are assuming that the Russians would respond to our moral lead because they share with the rest of us some manifest desire to do the right thing by humanity. I can see no reason for thinking that the Soviet government, or any militant government with enormous power in its hands, has ever acted or would ever act like that.

KENNAN: We have to lead step by step, and unless there is response, there can be no more concessions for the moment from our side. But you must realise that at the back of this whole great question of military competition, there is an even greater question which people very seldom ask themselves.

We are faced with two conceivable versions of catastrophe. One is a possible, but by no means certain, catastrophe in case we should militarily clash with the Russians. The other is an absolutely certain ecological and demographic disaster which is going to overtake this planet within the next, I would say, 60–70 years, but the effects of which will probably make themselves very painfully felt before the end of this century. The second of these two, if allowed to develop, may be final—there can be no real recovery from it. It is possible that some parts of humanity may survive it; but this would, at best, mean the beginning of a new Dark Age—all we have achieved in Western civilisation over the last 2,000 years would be lost.

In the face of this crisis, which is predictable and now almost inevitable, how can we be so absorbed with the one that is not inevitable—that is to say, the nuclear conflict with Russia—that we concentrate all our energies on the latter? Compared to the dangers which confront us on the ecological and demographic front, the possibility of Soviet control of Western Europe, even if one thought that this was a likely thing to happen (which I don't) would strike me as a minor catastrophe. After all, people *do live* in the Soviet Union. For the mass of people there, life is not intolerable. The same is true in East Germany; the same is true in Hungary. It is not what these people would like; but, still, it is a way of living, and it does not mean the end of the experiment of human civilisation; it leaves the way open for further developments. But from the ecological catastrophe that looms in front of us there is no recovery.

We have been putting the emphasis in the wrong places. We talk of saving Western civilisation when we talk of a military confrontation with Russia—but, saving it for what? In order that 20 or 30 years hence we may run out of oil, and minerals, and food, and invite upon humanity a devastating conflict between the over-populated and undernourished two-thirds of the world and ourselves?

URBAN: You have now put forward two powerful reasons for thinking that our concern to save Western civilisation from any real or imaginary Soviet threat is misplaced and indeed erroneous. One is the decadence of the West: the disintegration of the moral fibre of society in Western Europe, and the inability of the United States to offer anything worth learning to the rest of the world. Your second reasoning claims that our entire preoccupation with the danger of Soviet expansionism rests on a false conception of priorities: the ecological disaster will be a certain disaster whereas the Soviet threat is contingent—it will probably never materialise, and if it does, we can survive it.

It does seem to me that the West cannot win in terms of either of your scenarios. Moreover, I would infer from the moral thrust of your reasoning that your tacit message is not only that the West cannot win, but that it doesn't deserve to win.

You have come a long way from advocating, as you did in *American Diplomacy* (1951), a policy of firm containment, designed to confront the Russians with unalterable counterforce at every point where they show signs of encroaching upon the interest of a peaceful and stable world.

Are you now really saying that the amount of freedom that exists, for example, in Hungary or Poland is enough to put these basically totalitarian states on a par with Holland or Britain, so much so that the whole concept of the defence of Western civilisation is rendered hollow and (in the face of the possibility of an ecological catastrophe) essentially meaningless?

KENNAN: Of course not. The differences exist and they are important. The decline of the West is not a fully accomplished fact, nor is our stumbling into this great physical catastrophe final. If we in the West could get over this fixation we have with the idea that the Russians are dying to drop bombs on us, and think, instead, of what is happening to our planet, and address ourselves, resolutely and rapidly, to preventing the catastrophe that looms before us, we would be doing a great deal better. You must remember that as far as the pollution of the earth is concerned, this is largely the work of the great industrial nations which are spread out around the fertile zones of the northern hemisphere. If they could be induced to behave differently, we would have a breathing space. Otherwise we are going to face irrevocable disaster. Aren't we, then (to repeat something that can never be repeated often enough) being unrealistic in the amount of attention we devote to protecting ourselves from the Russians who, God knows, are not ten feet tall, who have all sorts of troubles of their own, who can't run an agricultural system that really works, who can't adequately house their population, who are rapidly losing their prestige and leadership in the World Communist movement, and have to reckon with China on their long frontier in the East? Isn't it grotesque to spend so much of our energy on opposing such a Russia in order to save a West which is honeycombed with bewilderment and a profound sense of internal decay?

Show me first an America which has successfully coped with the problems of crime, drugs, deteriorating educational standards, urban decay, pornography, and decadence of one sort or another—show me an America that has pulled itself together and is what it ought to be, then I will tell you how we are going to defend ourselves from the Russians. But as things are, I can see very little merit in organising ourselves to defend from the Russians the porno-shops in central Washington. In fact, the Russians are much better in holding pornography at bay than we are.

Please understand that, for purposes of argument, I am given to overstating a case; and that is one of the reasons why you accuse me of contradiction. If one wants to see both sides of a coin, one has, momentarily at least, to bring out each side in exaggerated relief.

URBAN: This is also one of the useful hazards of the dialogue, and I am, as you may have noticed to your dismay, myself far from unwilling to overstate a case in order to press home a point.

Your attitude to the defence of the West seems to have undergone a profound change in the last quarter of a century, and possibly even in the last six or seven years, because the passages I am about to cite, although dating back to 1949, were quoted by you with, I must assume, approval in 1968, in the first volume of your *Memoirs*.

Here then we have a very different estimate of the worth of Western civilisation, and a very different guidance as to how we ought to go about defending ourselves against dictatorships.

The year is 1949; you are revisiting the war-ravaged city of Hamburg which you had known and admired before the war, and this is what you say:

> . . . it suddenly appeared to me that in these ruins there was an unanswerable symbolism which we in the West could not afford to ignore. If the Western world was really going to make valid the pretence of a higher moral departure point . . . then it had to learn to fight its wars morally as well as militarily, or not fight them at all; for moral principles were part of its strength. Shorn of this strength, it was no longer itself; its victories were no real victories; and the best it would accomplish in the long run would be to pull down the temple over its own head. The military would stamp this as naivety; they would say that war is war, that when you're in it you fight with every means you have, or go down in defeat. But if that is the case, then there rests upon Western civilisation, bitter as this may be, the obligation to be militarily stronger than its adversaries by a margin sufficient to enable it to dispense with those means which can stave off defeat only at the cost of undermining victory.

This is an impressive passage, and it does seem to suggest that the Western democracies, precisely because they are essentially defensive polities, must be militarily superior to a potential aggressor (1) to deter him, and (2) if the deterrent does not work, to defeat him quickly and decisively.

KENNAN: There may be a certain inconsistency here. But don't forget that the words you cited were written 27 years ago, and even then they were predicated on: "*If* the Western world was really going to make valid the pretence of a higher moral departure point. . . ." Now everything I have said in this conversation goes towards showing that we have not at all been able to make that pretence valid.

My second point is that I have never been averse to the maintenance of strong conventional forces—what I am averse to are the weapons of mass destruction. Now this may strike you as a feeble explanation, and I can see ways in which it could be attacked. But, human nature being what it is, it would be idle to demand that wars of every sort should henceforth be outlawed. One has to keep a sense of relativity about wars and be content to ask that no one should be allowed to engage in wars of mass destruction.

You know how the Chinese used to fight their battles. They would march up with great screaming and blowing of bugles, and beating of drums, and flying of flags; and when they had figured out which side had the stronger forces, victory would be conceded to that side without shooting, which saved the face of the defeated party—and then both sides would march back to where they had started.

URBAN: 18th-century Europe saw a number of limited wars which were not much more destructive. I'm reminded of Defoe's famous observation: "Now it is frequent to have armies of fifty thousand men of a side at bay within view of another, and spend a whole campaign in dodging, or, as it is genteelly called, observing one another, and then march off into winter quarters." And the Earl of Chesterfield, writing in 1757: ". . . even war is pusillanimously carried on in this degenerate age; quarter is given; towns are taken, and the people spared; even in a storm, a woman can hardly hope for the benefit of a rape."

KENNAN: The 18th century was highly civilised. Today, the intricacies of nuclear strategy and the abstruse theology about "MIRVing" and "throw-weights" would be much better understood if they were seen for what, in fact, they are: symbolic, or, if you like, prophylactic enactments of battles which will never be fought. And the reason they cannot be so regarded at the present time—and I'm coming back to a point I have already made—is that Western Europe has, wrongly and unfortunately, chosen to be dependent on the American nuclear arsenal and is thus unwilling to put up conventional forces of sufficient strength to defend itself. Nor do I just mean that Western Europe ought to provide itself with more tanks, and rockets, and fighter planes. There was something in my Reith Lectures for which I was more ridiculed, and for which I found less understanding, than anything I ever said in my life. This related to the concept of national defence through passive resistance—the concept of making it impossible for a foreign occupier to run a conquered country. Everyone laughed at me. There was a debate in the German *Bundestag*. Willy Brandt was there—"Well," he said, "you must allow every man some foolish ideas. . . ."

I did not, of course, mean that one could erode the power of an occupier in Western Europe by relying exclusively on civil disobedience. But I did think that if a reasonable degree of conventional armaments could be supported by a trained and disciplined civilian population, one need never resort to the use of nuclear weapons.

URBAN: What you are advocating is guerrilla warfare.

KENNAN: Yes, if you will, but guerrilla war for defence.

URBAN: A Chinese-Vietnamese type of resistance.

KENNAN: Yes, and this kind of thing was done in World War II. But whereas the wartime European underground was improvised very late in the game and with great and unnecessary losses, the underground I have in mind would be well prepared and probably more effective. I can see no objection to this at all. I have been closely associated with a village where I live near Harrisburg [Pennsylvania]; if we had a foreign occupier and the people of the village said: "Let's make up a band, and try to defend ourselves"—I would go with them. This would not be doing anything terrible to anybody—this would be merely trying to protect the fabric of one's life.

URBAN: Your own little war of national liberation, in fact.

KENNAN: Yes, if you will; but look at the alternatives. Let us suppose there were to be a nuclear attack of some sort on this country and millions of people were killed and injured. Let us further suppose that we had the ability to retaliate against the urban centres of the country that had attacked us. Would you want to do that? I wouldn't. Granted we had suffered this catastrophe, it would give me no pleasure to know that we followed it up by burning up two or three million civilians in some other great city in the world.

URBAN: You are a great gentleman—but the world is not cast in your image. My suspicion is that the plain people in Columbus, Ohio, might take intense pleasure if a Soviet city were incinerated in retaliation for an American; indeed, they might very well demand it. Wasn't the British night-bombing of German cities during the last War very largely a similar exercise, openly undertaken on the strength of the argument that the bombing would maintain British and depress German civilian morale—for the damage it was doing to the German war machine was rather minimal?

KENNAN: I have no high opinion of human beings: they are always going to fight and do nasty things to each other. They are always going to be part animal, governed by their emotions and subconscious drives rather than by reason. They will always, as Freud remarked, feel a grave *Unbehagen*, a discomfort, at having to live in a civilised framework, and kick against it. But if that is so, the only thing you can do with them is to see that the weapons they have are not too terrible. You must prevent them from playing with the worst kind of toys. This is why I feel that the great weapons of mass-destruction—and nuclear arms are not the only conceivable ones—should never be in human hands, that it would be much better to go back, symbolically speaking, to bows and arrows which at least do not destroy nature. I have no sympathy with the man who demands an eye for an eye in a nuclear conflict.

I would be much happier for my children (and this is, again, one of those overstatements which I must ask you not to take too literally for I could argue against it) if we had no nuclear weapons at all—if we were in the position of Norway which has no nuclear arms, or in the position of Mexico. The Norwegians and Mexicans have a chance. Bear in mind that if there is an incentive for the Soviet Government, or any other nuclear power, to use these weapons against us, it must be sought in the fact that we are ourselves developing them—only fear could lead anybody to do anything so monstrous.

URBAN: But is it fear alone? Might it not be the lure of quick victory, or the megalomania of a dictator with his eyes on the main chance?

KENNAN: A nuclear strike would not be a rational action for any government.

URBAN: Are governments always rational? If the actions of ordinary human beings are, as you say, suffused with subconscious drives and other forms of the irrational, I cannot see how one could convincingly argue that the actions of governments, which are made up of the same human material, are subject to different rules. For example, Khrushchev's Cuban venture, to stay within our recent experience, was close to being an irrational act of policy.

KENNAN: We had put weapons into Turkey and many other places close to the Soviet borders, and Khrushchev thought he could, by stationing his missiles in Cuba, develop bargaining power to induce us to withdraw our stuff from Turkey. And although his action did, as it turned out, take us pretty close to a conflict, he did more or less achieve what he had set out to.

You see, I don't view the Soviet leaders as monsters who want to commit great acts of destruction purely for the sake of destruction. They are Marxists whose political purpose undoubtedly requires the spread of their ideology and the expansion of Soviet power; they feel they are on a course of intellectual and political ascendancy—but I don't think the wanton destruction of large numbers of people fits in with their purpose. This is not the Marxist line at all. If they use the Bomb on us, they destroy workers together with the bourgeoisie. What sense would that make?

3. How Right the Old Kennan Was!

Hugh Seton-Watson

✫ ✫ ✫ ✫ ✫ ✫ ✫ ✫ ✫ ✫ ✫ ✫ ✫ ✫ ✫ ✫

In direct response to Ambassador Kennan's views expressed in the conversation with George Urban (see selection 2), Professor Seton-Watson, a well-reputed British expert on the Soviet Union and Eastern Europe, charges Kennan with confusing utopia with reality. Kennan's new utopianism, he says, is seized with "an obsession to compare the state of existing societies with some imaginary perfection," and thus it leads to irresponsible policy advice.

Mr. Seton-Watson, while agreeing with "a large part" of Mr. Kennan's argument, finds himself in profound disagreement with the latter's assessment of the dangers confronting the West: "I do not believe that the dangers of pollution, crime, drugs and moral decadence are more urgent or more menacing than the danger of Soviet imperialism."

Professor Seton-Watson teaches at the School of Slavonic and Eastern European Studies of the University of London.

✫ ✫ ✫ ✫ ✫ ✫ ✫ ✫ ✫ ✫ ✫ ✫ ✫ ✫ ✫ ✫

Excerpted by permission from "George Kennan's Illusions: A Reply," published in *Encounter*, November 1976.

GEORGE KENNAN MAKES THE DISTURBING ASSERTION that the United States has so patently failed to solve its internal problems in the past 20–30 years that it has nothing to offer the world by way of example. It is, he argues (ENCOUNTER, September), particularly grotesque for the United States to spend so much of its energy on opposing a much weakened Soviet Russia

> in order to save a West which is honeycombed with bewilderment and a profound sense of internal decay. . . . Show me first an America which has successfully coped with the problems of crime, drugs, deteriorating educational standards, urban decay, pornography, and decadence of one sort or another—show me an America that has pulled itself together and is what it ought to be, then I will tell you how we are going to defend ourselves from the Russians.

The attitude Kennan represents suffers from a utopian fallacy. People have, of course, always had utopian aspirations; but these were, in the past, for the most part confined to literature. In our own times, something entirely new has happened: it has become an obsession to compare the state of existing societies with some imaginary perfection, and to draw practical conclusions from the gap between what is and what could be.

Previous effective cultures did not ask themselves this sort of question. They did not believe that perfection was attainable by mortal beings; and where they did ask this question, they had religious answers to it—either to the effect that these problems were for the next life, for God and not for man, or else (as in the case of Buddhism) that perfection lay in a substanceless, perpetual motion in which everyone could, as an individual, become his own Buddha. But to set up a model of perfection on earth, and then to say: "We don't conform to this pattern," is a disease of modern times; and it is one which has become very widespread through the media, which Kennan rightly criticises.

Take the history of the American republic. It has its horrors, its crimes, and its glories, and often they are tied up together. Or take the American Civil War; in some ways it was glorious, in some ways it was odious. The Black problem, the problem of slavery, has been with America since the beginning. Who could solve it? One might say there should never have been a slave trade. True, there never *should* have been; but there was, historically, and its consequences are still alive. Tremendous efforts have been made, both by whites and blacks, to better the black man's lot; great successes have been achieved. Yet each success creates its own frustrations.

Crime—yes, there does seem to be more crime; and there is a drug disease in modern society; and I would not disagree with Kennan that these things must be fought and eliminated. But to say that, because all this exists, a society does not deserve to be defended, seems to me grotesque. This is not how nations, societies, and cultures have operated in the past. They worked; they defended themselves; they produced good and bad rulers, reformers and people resistant to reform; they grew and struggled and declined. And when they finally collapsed, it was because there was a combination of pressures from outside, and a loss of self-confidence by the educated class itself. This seems to me to be the disease that is present today particularly in Britain (it is, under the surface, just as bad in France) and widespread in the United States. While denouncing this phenomenon, Kennan seems, in a sense, to be exemplifying it. Surely states do not exist for the purpose of bringing about perfection on earth.

Kennan is right in saying that the American polity and American history are peculiar to the circumstances in which the United States was born, and can never be repeated. But all that means is that America is a very peculiar polity and society which has some defects that the rest of us don't have, and some great virtues. Take it as it is; it has warts and it has beauty. It has strengths and weaknesses. It does stupid things at times; many of its spokesmen are third-rate people, but politicians of all states include many mediocrities. Some of them say ridiculous things; some do nasty things. But why, for that reason, should one be ridden with guilt and cry: "What has America to offer to the world? . . . What utopian panacea can it provide? . . ." And if it cannot provide them—is it guilty? This seems to me an unhistorical way of looking at history.

A Model for Mankind?

Did the United States ever claim that the American experience had universal validity? Did the American model become, at the height of American power, an American socio-cultural imperialism? There arose in the late 19th century, in the European environment of expanding industrialisation, a new social élite in all major countries, with a certain, brash self-confidence—a belief that they knew how to run the world; and the Americans were only one example. But in those days the validity of one's "model" was not felt to impose on one the duty of imposing the model on other peoples.

The French may have believed that the French language and culture were the only ones that could really be called a civilisation, but (with the only partial exception of Napoleon) Frenchmen did not attempt to foist it on others. The idea of spreading one's culture around the world was more characteristic of the last part of the 19th century when Germany, and Russia too, began to feel that they had "models" to offer to the rest of mankind.

All this is disappearing now because the heirs to 19th-century European imperialism are riddled with guilt-complexes. It has survived only in one place—the Soviet Union. The paradox is that, although, of all the 19th-century imperialist élites, the one that was weakest was precisely the Russian élite—and although the élite was destroyed as such in the Revolution (though individual members of it of course survived)—yet now, nearly sixty years after the Bolshevik Revolution, a new Russian élite has been found; and not only is it full of imperial arrogance, but there is a quite specific continuity of style between its imperial arrogance and the old. The truth is that the recruitment of a new élite to run Stalin's industrialisation programmes produced a caste of formidable, self-righteous, expansive caricatures of the brash 19th-century Western imperialist—of a Theodore Roosevelt and a Joseph Chamberlain.

American supremacy in the world in the 1940s and 1950s did not have this socio-cultural characteristic. The Americans saw what was happening in the territories that the Soviet Union was occupying, and they reacted to what they saw. Up to the Communist takeover of Eastern and Central Europe there had been a tremendous enthusiasm for the Russians as allies and for the Soviet Union as a new social order. The Russians were fighting bravely against Hitler, and they had something splendid to offer. Roosevelt felt this, and so did millions of Americans. Then they saw that once Russians were on top, they began brutally to oppress the European peoples whom they had conquered. There grew up a feeling that this had to be stopped, and the way to stop it was to give the old and still strong European nations the opportunity to defend themselves. The Marshall Plan was set in train, and the tables were turned. But to say that the Marshall Plan expressed a missionary zeal to "Americanise Europe"—or that it was a piece of "American imperialism"—is complete nonsense. There was none of that arrogant moralising to shape the world in one's image that is characteristic of Soviet expansionism. But there *was* a belief that it was the Americans' duty to stand up for liberty. That kind of idealism was certainly behind the Marshall Plan and the founding of NATO. It does not seem to me at all a discreditable motivation.

Kennan insists that, before we can effectively defend ourselves against the Soviet Union, we have to learn how to defend ourselves from our own sinfulness.

Nothing can defend a society from itself if its upper 100,000 men and women, both the decision-makers and those who help to mould the thinking of the decision-makers, are resolved to capitulate. Perhaps there was something of that in the collapse of the Roman Empire and the rise on its ruins of the barbarian kingdoms. Sitting back comfortably in the year 1976, we can say: "Well, the Roman Empire itself wasn't all that worthy of respect. It collapsed in the 5th century, but by about 1100 A.D. a combination of Barbarian, Roman and Christian inheritance had created a splendid mediaeval civilisation. . . ." It is rather easy to talk like that; but 700 years is a very long time, and to wish on our descendants for generations on end a barbarism no less brutal than, although different from, that of the Frankish barbarians, seems to me a criminally frivolous attitude to take.

Silence in the West

This Soviet colonialism, victimising nearly two hundred million Europeans and nearly fifty million Asians, is something that Western governments and Western mass media have kept quiet about for most of the time in the last twenty years. There have been occasional exceptions—at the time of the Hungarian Revolution in 1956 and the Prague Spring in 1968—and every now and then someone at the United Nations has uttered a few words about the Soviet Empire in Asia. But these have been flashes in the pan. For twenty years and more, spokesmen of Communist-controlled governments have poured forth anti-imperialist rhetoric and abuse against Western governments (which have given independence to one Asian and African territory after another), and have worked uninterruptedly—and rather successfully—to get the spokesmen of these Asian and African governments to join in the chorus. And all the time the Western spokesmen in the United Nations have sat there and said nothing. Why? . . .

Of course, when one says this sort of thing, one hears at once parrot-cries about confrontation. One must not weaken détente—or provoke Soviet anger—by telling the truth. But why not? Does détente mean unending and unlimited liberty for the Soviets to vilify, to exaggerate, and to revile us for crimes and errors (and, of course, we have plenty to feel guilty about), and also to invent other crimes which we never committed . . . but no liberty at all for anybody to say anything about their crimes? Are "offences against détente" by definition only Western acts?

I am not asking for confrontation; I am not suggesting that we should fly 12,000 Chilean troops across the ocean to join an Uzbek liberation movement in Soviet Central Asia. I am asking a simple question: why is it that we go on with this moral and political disarming of our own peoples (and of the New Nations) by not telling the truth about the Soviet empire?

One further point. The Soviet rulers allowed the Finns to rule themselves the way they wanted—no Finnish Communist dictatorship, and no falsification of Finnish history or Finnish culture. Now perhaps it would be too big a risk for the Soviet leaders to allow the Poles and Czechs as much liberty as the Finns have; and if they did, they might find the Estonians and Ukrainians and Georgians asking for the same thing. But at least they could stop this squalid business of national humiliation; of distorting national culture and traditions, of making proud peoples perform ritual kowtows towards superior Russian civilisation. This at least would go some of the way towards taking the detonators out of the explosive material which is piled up in Central and Eastern Europe. These set off small explosions in 1956 and 1968, and will certainly set off more in the future—when we cannot be sure that the effect will be limited, as it was in those years.

This is also the Soviet interest, not just ours. But it is something that only they can do, not we. We can't get the Poles to accept indefinite national humiliation; the Poles are not ours to hand over. Helsinki could not and did not change that, and this could be something that we might explain to the Russians and help them to understand. How and when—how much by public speaking and how much by secret diplomacy—is a matter which the professionals should have views about; that is what nations employ the professionals for. But my impression is that no one is even thinking about this.

But wouldn't our outspokenness about Eastern Europe risk unleashing rebellion there? It didn't in 1956; it was Stalinism—Russification, the AVO Secret Police and Rakosi's brutalitarianism—that made the Hungarians rise, not the words of President Eisenhower or Foster Dulles. The threat of upheavals and war comes from Soviet repression, not from the fact that we talk about it. The Soviet leaders themselves must be made to realise that it is their policy of antagonising the East European nations that is creating the danger for them—a danger which surely some Soviet leaders would genuinely like to escape, and it is up to us to help them to do so. The essential truth is that Soviet policy manufactures rebellion. It is the humiliation of historic nations, as distinct from mere domination by a powerful neighbour, that creates fatal resentments. This policy has turned the middle of Europe into a powder magazine.

I haven't answered Kennan's question: "What should our policy be to Eastern Europe?" I can't come up with a magic formula, but I'm sure we must show that we realise the realities and must go on saying so. We must be neither timid nor naive, and here one can quote Kennan against Kennan—the old Kennan, who was extremely critical of Roosevelt's infantile trust of Stalin, against the new Kennan as he appears in ENCOUNTER'S "From Containment . . . to Self-Containment." How right the old Kennan was! And how much the old Kennan's attitude is, *mutatis mutandis*, still the only appropriate one for us to take!

Unilateral Nuclear Disarmament

Kennan's anxiety to avoid the threat of a nuclear holocaust leads him close to advocating unilateral American nuclear disarmament and the gradual withdrawal of United States forces from Europe.

I don't go along with him on that. I am convinced that the present rulers of the Soviet Union are determined to have the entire range of weapons to fight every kind of war there can be, from local wars to the all-out nuclear conflict. They believe that, in the last resort, they can win a nuclear war, and that the world that comes out of the ruins will be one they will control.

Of course, when Kennan says that no government would willingly start a nuclear war, I agree with him: it *is* difficult to believe that one would. But given a sufficient degree of American disarmament, and enough political and military retreats, a situation might arise in which the Soviet Government, with its eyes on the main chance, might conclude that a nuclear ultimatum would produce results. If it did, that would (for the time being anyhow) be the end of the matter. But if it did not, it would then find itself boxed into a corner where it would have to use nuclear weapons or lose face and credibility.

But there is another kind of situation which worries me more because it is less improbable. European demarcation lines being firm, it is very unlikely that war will break out in Europe in the foreseeable future. But there are many other parts of the world where there are no such lines. Consider the dangers implicit in the Cuban invasion of Angola—this terrifying spectacle of 12,000 highly trained and heavily armed troops being transported in Russian aircraft across the Atlantic Ocean, right under the nose of the United States, and getting away with it. It isn't a matter of rights and wrongs in Angola. It is certainly not a matter of whether Vorster's treatment of the Blacks is unjust or not—it obviously is unjust. But the spectacle of an odious imperialist power spreading its tentacles without serious repercussions frightens me.

What I am afraid of is that a situation might occur in which Soviet or Soviet-sponsored forces were so deeply committed that the Americans would suddenly be jolted into realising what was going on: "Good God, we can't afford to let this happen. . . ." They would then start reacting clumsily, and guns would go off.

I am reminded of Germany before the first World War. The old doctrine that World War I was brought about by the wicked imperialism of a sinister Hohenzollern William II is obviously nonsense. Another doctrine which says that the War was due to the "conflicting interests of British and German capitalism" is equally ill-founded; there were all kinds of conflicts among the great powers which played a causal part.

But something of great consequence happened between the departure of Bismarck and the outbreak of the war in 1914. A process set in which made certain conflicts, which had already been there but had been manageable by statesmen like Bismarck, entirely unmanageable. And that process was the appearance of an arrogant state of mind in a large section of the German public (it was symbolised by the Kaiser, though by no means created by him). If you look for one social class which was more to blame for this rising arrogance than any other, it was my own class—academics, *gymnasium* teachers, and university lecturers. German spokesmen, led by the Emperor, were beating their fists on the table whenever there was a minor international crisis: "Germany will be heard . . . Germany is a *Weltmacht* . . . we will make ourselves felt everywhere," until the other European governments began to be worried and had to ask themselves: "What are these people going to do next?"

This arrogant rise of a parvenu power, with tremendous national forces at its disposal, is exactly what we are seeing today in the shape of Soviet hegemony spreading to the South Atlantic and the Indian Ocean. It is symbolised by the attitude of people like Marshal Grechko and all the other Soviet mailed-fist bullies, both civilian politicians and generals.

Khrushchev, with all his brashness, was not like this, much less Stalin (who had a minor touch of Bismarck about him—a dangerous enemy, certainly, but a very cool, self-controlled man who took no risks). But this new class of Soviet imperialists frightens me. If there is a danger of war in the world today, it comes from their aggressiveness, and from the reaction they are sooner or later bound to provoke.

Ranking the Dangers

To summarise, I agree with a large part of George Kennan's argument; and I believe that he agrees with me about the unity of Europe as a cultural concept—a unity which cannot be confined to the Carolingian lands, nor exclude the misnamed "Easterners." But the one deep difference between us concerns the priority of the dangers with which Europeans and Americans alike are faced.

I do not believe that the dangers of pollution, crime, drugs and moral decadence (all of which I recognise as very serious and very pressing) are more urgent or more menacing than the danger of Soviet imperialism. The Russians, I agree, are not "going to drop atom bombs on us." Soviet Russia, I agree, has a backward economy, a miserable agriculture, and an obsolete bureaucratic mechanism whose joints creak with rust and old age. But the rulers of the USSR have vast military power; assign an overriding priority to increasing their armed forces of all types; and are themselves driven by a combination of armour-plated self-righteousness, will to power, and lust for more power over more people, which make them extremely formidable. It remains their purpose to impose their antiquated form of tyranny on every new victim which comes within their reach. Whether armed force has to be used, or whether submission can be obtained by threats and subversion, is for them a matter not of principle but of expediency. Whenever they meet with no counterforce, material or moral, with no will to self-defence, they advance. There is no sign at all that their attitude is changing, or that the younger *apparatchiks* who will succeed them are made of milder stuff.

It is no doubt true that the societies of the West have more sophisticated economies, technologies, intelligentsias, and more sophisticated forms of consumption and pleasure. None of these will help them if they give a low priority to their own defence (political and moral, no less than economic and military) or fail to distinguish between friend and foe.

The crocodile is a more primitive zoological specimen than the human being; but if a man steps blindfold and naked into a crocodile's river, it is the crocodile who will prevail.

4. Soviet Doves and American Hawks

George F. Kennan

✫ ✫ ✫ ✫ ✫ ✫ ✫ ✫ ✫ ✫ ✫ ✫ ✫ ✫ ✫ ✫

In his November 22, 1977, speech before a Council on Foreign Relations session in Washington, D.C., Mr. Kennan insisted that there has been drastic transformation in the Soviet Union since the time of Stalin, from an insecure and blustering leadership to a more confident and moderate one.

He characterizes the new Soviet leadership as "highly conservative" with a horror of war and not given to "rash adventure" — "men more seriously concerned to preserve the present limits of their political power and responsibility than to expand those limits — men whose motivation is essentially defensive and whose attention is riveted primarily to the unsolved problems of economic development within their own country." In their own interests they want "a peaceful and constructive relationship with the United States."

Such a relationship, says Kennan, is menaced by a "hardline opposition" group in the United States which has "the power to veto any Soviet-American agreements in the military or the economic field that do not meet its requirements." These "military enthusiasts" see the U.S.-Soviet relationship "exclusively as one of military rivalry."

Mr. Kennan says this obstructionist "effort from the Right" is profoundly misguided because it persists in regarding the Soviet Union as a threat to the United States and its interests. We cannot afford to permit these people to "torpedo any agreements" on arms limitations with the Soviet Union. We must, he concludes, develop a consensus by laying aside, at least for the moment, "the whole question of the military relationship," and by humbly examining new realities in the Soviet Union.

✫ ✫ ✫ ✫ ✫ ✫ ✫ ✫ ✫ ✫ ✫ ✫ ✫ ✫ ✫ ✫

Reprinted by permission from *The Washington Post*, December 11, 1977; the article appeared there under the title "A Plea by Mr. X 30 Years Later."

JUST 60 YEARS AGO there came into being the present political regime in Russia. And exactly at the halfway point of that span of time—30 years ago—I chanced to deliver a talk on the subject of Soviet-American relations which became the basis for an article in the magazine Foreign Affairs signed by the pseudonym "X." This article attained a certain melancholy notoriety and has dogged my footsteps ever since, like a faithful, but unwanted and somewhat embarrassing animal.

The coincidence of chronology naturally leads me to reflect on the changes that have occurred since that year of 1947 in the background against which Soviet-American relations have had to proceed. The Russian political scene was then dominated by a single great personality—a man whom Churchill very aptly called a "crafty giant"—a man of enormous political-tactical genius—a formidable opponent on anyone's terms, but one whose combination of paranoia with cruelty and political mastery had served to create one of the great totalitarian monstrosities of our time: a personal despotism as ruthless and far-reaching as anything the modern world has ever known. By 1947 this despotism had already cost the Soviet peoples several millions of lives. And it had not stopped at the old Russian borders but had been extended—and this with our tacit blessing—to nearly one-half of the remainder of the European continent. And no one could be sure, in 1947, that it would stop there.

The danger was not one of further military conquest. (Actually, it never has been that.) The problem was that Western Europe, still dazed, shaken and jittery from the effects of the Hitlerian conquest, did not know what to expect. Its peoples lacked confidence in themselves. They had a tendency to rush for safety to the side of whoever they thought was likely to win in the end. They would have been quite capable of throwing themselves into the arms of their own Communist parties if they gained the impression that those Communist parties represented the wave of the future. And to this had to be added the fact that the Moscow center, and Stalin personally, enjoyed at that time a total monopolistic control over the world Communist movement—a control which meant that any success by any Communist party anywhere in seizing power within its own country had to be regarded as equivalent in its effects to a military conquest by the Soviet Union.

It is enough to cite these circumstances, I think, to make clear the magnitude of the changes that have occurred in this 30-year interval. The Soviet Union remains, of course, an authoritarian state—much as was the prerevolutionary Tsarist Russia; but there is very little to be seen today of the terror that prevailed in Stalin's time; and the regime is headed by a moderate, in fact conservative man; a man who, whatever other failings of outlook he may have, is a man of the middle, a skilled balancer among political forces—a man confidently regarded by all who know him as a man of peace.

Moscow's monopoly of authority over the world Communist movement has been thoroughly disrupted—so much so that even in the case of those Communist parties that still ostensibly recognize the Soviet leadership, the lines of authority leading from Moscow are tenuous and incapable of bearing much weight. It is a case where the semblance of authority can be retained only by the sacrifice of much of the reality.

And finally, in place of the anxious, jittery Western Europe of 1947 we now have an area which is unquestionably the seat of some of the most successful civilization, economically and socially, that the modern world has to show. The change, to be sure, has not been complete. People have not fully overcome the trauma of two world wars. Many still lack confidence in themselves, see dangers on every hand, require to be reassured periodically, like frightened children. This situation has its military implications, and plays a part, of course, in Soviet-American relations. But it cannot be compared in seriousness and dangerousness to the situation we faced in 1947.

The Ambiguity of Detente

Now all these changes, and others I might cite, have run in the direction of an improvement in the objective possibilities for a better Soviet-American relationship. This does not mean, of course, possibilities for a complete normalization of those relations. For that there remain too many obstacles—historical, psychological and ideological. There has always been, and remains today, an area in which no complete political intimacy is possible, where interests must remain competitive and in part conflicting.

But there is also another area, an area in which interests largely coincide and limited collaboration is possible. In the light of the changes we have just had occasion to note, this latter area has tended, slowly but steadily, to grow. And where sensible efforts have been put forward on both sides to take advantage of this situation—where people have tried, in other words, to create a balanced, businesslike and realistic relationship between two very disparate political systems—the results, given patience and persistence, have not been discouraging.

This was true, among others, in the period of the Nixon-Kissinger detente. Progress was made in a number of fields which was more than negligible and from which both sides are continuing to benefit today. The fact that these achievements were somewhat overdramatized, that they led to unreal expectations and gave rise to some disillusionment when these expectations were not met, should not blind us to their positive residue.

Nevertheless, the effort to pursue a balanced and useful middle course in the relationship with Russia has never been an easy one for American policy-makers to follow; and one of the main reasons why this has been so difficult is that seldom, if ever, have we had an adequate consensus in American opinion on the nature of the problem and the most promising ways of approaching it.

Prior to the late 1940s—prior, that is, to the Korean War and the death of Stalin—the difficulty seemed to come primarily from the left: from people who had a naive, overtrusting, overidealistic view of what was then Stalinist power—people who thought it really possible for this country to ingratiate itself with the Stalin regime by various one-sided gestures of confidence and generosity and reproached our government for not doing so. It was, incidentally, against this sort of left-wing deviation that the "X article," and the policy of containment, were directed.

But since Stalin's death, the opposition to an even-handed and realistic policy toward Russia has tended to come from the opposite end of the political spectrum: from people who were unable to see the curious mix of the negative and the positive, of the discouraging and the hopeful, in the Soviet political personality—people who could see only the negative, and who feared the consequences of anything less than a total rejection and hostility from our side.

There has never been a time in these last 25 years, it seems to me, when this opposition has not made itself felt. There has never been a time when American statesmen concerned to find and develop a constructive middle-ground in relations with Russia have not felt their efforts harassed from this direction.

And the harassment has not been minor in intensity or in power. Every administration has been to some extent afraid of this hard-line opposition. It had behind it the power of chauvinist rhetoric as well as that of strict military logic. It had the capability of hurling at any and all opponents the charge of being "soft on communism"; and however meaningless this phrase may be, it is a formidable weapon in a society unhappily vulnerable to the power of the slogan.

In the heyday of the Nixon-Kissinger detente, this opposition was almost silenced—partly by Richard Nixon's formidable credentials as a hard-liner, which bewildered many critics; and partly by Henry Kissinger's diplomatic fireworks, which dazzled them. But the resulting silence was one of frustration, not of acceptance. When Watergate drained the authority of this political combination, the opposition broke forth once again with redoubled strength and violence. It has raged over the entire period from 1975 to the present. It sufficed to knock out the 1974 trade agreement and to lower the level of Soviet-American trade. It sufficed to delay the approach to a new SALT agreement. And it has achieved today, against the background of a new administration and a somewhat unstructured Congress, a power it never had before. It now claims to have—and, for all I know, it does have—the power to veto any Soviet-American agreements in the military or the economic field that do not meet with its requirements; and such are its requirements that I come increasingly to suspect that this means, in effect, any conceivable agreements at all.

The Unreality of Military Planners

I have made my best efforts to understand the rationale of this opposition. Many of the bearers of it are my friends. I know them as honorable people. I do not suspect, or disrespect, their motives.

It is clear that we have to do here with a complex phenomenon, not a simple one. This body of opinion embraces some people whose trouble seems to be that they are unaware of the changes between 1947 and 1977, who talk of the problems of Soviet-American relations in terms identical with those used at the height of the Cold War—who sometimes seem, in fact, unaware that Stalin is dead.

Then, there are others whose emotions have been aroused over the question of human rights or Jewish emigration and who would like to see American policy directed not to an accommodation to Soviet power as it is but to the changing of the very nature of the Soviet regime.

More important, however, than either of these are the people who view the relationship exclusively as one of military rivalry—who see in it no significant values or issues or possibilities other than ones relating to the supposed determination of the Soviet leadership to achieve some sort of decisive military ascendancy over the NATO coalition—and this, of course, with the most menacing and deadly of intent.

These include outstandingly the military planners, whose professional obligation it is to set up a planner's dummy of any possible military opponent, to endow that dummy with just the motivation I have described, and then to treat it as if it were real. But this group also includes many non-military people who, accepting this dummy as the reality, lose themselves in the fantastic reaches of what I might call military mathematics—the mathematics of possible mutual destruction in an age of explosively burgeoning weapons technology.

Like many of the rest of you, I have made my efforts to understand the arguments of these military enthusiasts. I have tried to follow them through the mazes of their intricate and sophisticated calculations of possible military advantage at various future points in time. I have tried to follow them in their recital of the letters and numbers of various weapons systems, some real, some imagined, their comparisons of the reputed capacities of these systems, their computations of the interactions of them in situations of actual hostility.

I come away from this exercise frustrated, and with two overpowering impressions. The first is that this entire science of long-range massive destruction—of calculated advantage or disadvantage in modern weaponry—has gotten seriously out of hand; that the variables, the complexities, the uncertainties it involves are rapidly growing beyond the power of either human mind or computer.

But my second impression is that there is a distinct unreality about this whole science of destruction—unreality, that is, when you view it as the plane on which our differences over policy have to be resolved. I doubt that we are going to solve our problems by trying to agree as to whether the Russians will or will not have the capability of "taking out" our land-based missiles at some time in the 1980s. I doubt that this is the heart of the problem. I suspect that something deeper is involved. And if I had to try to define that deeper something, I would have to say that it is the view one takes of the nature of the Soviet leadership and of the discipline exerted upon it by its own experiences, problems and political necessities.

There are basically two views of this leadership: two ways in which it is seen in this country. In one of these views, the Soviet leaders appear as a terrible and forbidding group of men—monsters of sorts, really, because lacking in all elements of common humanity—men totally dedicated either to the destruction or to the political undoing and enslavement of this country and its allies—men who have all internal problems, whether of civic obedience or of economic development, essentially solved and are therefore free to spend their time evolving elaborate schemes for some ultimate military showdown—men who are prepared to accept the most tremendous risks, and to place upon their people the most fearful sacrifices, if only in this way their program of destruction or domination of ourselves and our allies can be successfully carried forward.

Soviet Leaders as 'Quite Ordinary Men'

That is one view. In the other view, these leaders are seen as a group of quite ordinary men, to some extent the victims, if you will, of the ideology on which they have been reared, but shaped far more importantly by the discipline of the responsibilities they and their predecessors have borne as rulers of a great country in the modern technological age. They are seen, in this view, as highly conservative men, perhaps the most conservative ruling group to be found anywhere in the world, markedly advanced in age, approaching the end of their tenure and given to everything else but rash adventure. They are seen as men who share the horror of major war that dominates most of the Soviet people, who have no desire to experience another military conflagration and no intention to launch one—men more seriously concerned to preserve the present limits of their political power and responsibility than to expand those limits—men whose motivation is essentially defensive and whose attention is riveted primarily to the unsolved problems of economic development within their own country. They are seen as men who suffer greatly under the financial burden which the maintenance of the present bloated arsenals imposes on the Soviet economy, and who would like to be relieved of that burden if this could be accomplished without undue damage to Russia's security and to their own political prestige. They are seen, finally, as men who are, to be sure, seldom easy to deal with, who care more about appearances than about reality, who have an unfortunate fixation about secrecy which complicates their external relations in many ways, but who, despite all these handicaps, have good and sound reason, rooted in their own interests, for desiring a peaceful and constructive relationship with the United States within the area where that is theoretically possible.

It is these two conflicting views of the Soviet leadership that lie at the heart of the conflict between those in our government who are attempting to make progress in our relations with the Soviet Union and those who are attacking this effort from the right. And the burden of what I have to say is that I think we can no longer permit this great conflict of outlook and opinion to go on in so large degree unreconciled as it has gone in recent years—that the moment has come when we can no longer carry on safely or effectively in our relations with the Soviet Union without the creation of a much wider consensus of opinion behind our policies of the moment than anything we have known in this recent period.

We stand at a crucial point in Soviet-American relations. The expiration of the 1972 SALT agreement has confronted us with fundamental decisions. Either we move forward, boldly, confidently and imaginatively, to the creation of a new relationship with that country in the military field, or we deliver up ourselves and the rest of the civilized world to the appalling dangers of a nuclear weapons race totally out of control—a development devoid of any visible hopeful end, devoid of any imaginable end at all other than a wholly disastrous and apocalyptic one.

But our ability to pursue the more hopeful of these alternatives is today seriously jeopardized by lack of the consensus to which I just referred. The opposition now being brought to bear against the efforts of the President and the Secretary of State to carry forward negotiations in the field of the limitation of armaments has reached a degree of intensity that seems to me to exceed anything we have known in the past. Powerful efforts are being made—the tendency of which is not to bring about the failure of ratification of instruments already negotiated (nobody could object to that as a matter of procedure) but to discredit the very process of negotiation, and this at a very early state. People are being attacked not for what they are known to have done in the negotiating process but for what they are presumed capable of doing—presumed capable on the basis of rumor or of calculated leak. They are being attacked, in other words, not for their actions but for their supposed intentions.

I am not questioning the motivation for these attacks. I can conceive that it may be, in many instances, of the highest. But I find myself wondering whether effective negotiations can be conducted in the face of opposition of this nature, particularly when we, as well as our Soviet counterparts, are being assured daily that the people who carry forward this opposition have not only the political power to torpedo any agreements or understandings that might realistically be arrived at, but also the firm intention to do so. Negotiating policy, it seems to me, cannot be effectively made or implemented against such a background.

And this present moment is one at which we simply cannot afford to have the force and momentum of our policy lamed in this manner. The stakes are too high. The penalties of failure are too serious. The implications of such a failure would carry even farther than just the prospect of an unlimited weapons race. A breakdown of the relationship on the military level could not fail to have—indeed, has already had to some extent—effects on other levels as well. And here, too, we have—and the world has—too much to lose to permit such a failure to occur.

We face in this coming period a tragically high probability of deepening crises in Southern Africa and in the Middle East. It may well be that the peace of the world will depend, as these crises develop, on the ability of the American and Soviet governments to remain in close communication, to give each other reasonable reassurance as to their intentions, and to coordinate their actions with a view to preventing local conflicts from growing to global dimensions.

Beyond this, we have the fact that these coming years are bound to see extensive changes in political leadership at the Soviet end. Nothing could be more unfortunate, surely, than that a new and inexperienced team of leaders should come into power in the Soviet Union confronting what would appear to be a blank wall of hostility and rejection at the American end—a situation in the face of which they would see no choice but to look for alternatives other than those of good relations with the United States. This is no time to foreclose other people's options, and particularly not the options of people new to the experience of power and obliged to define new lines of policy that may represent commitments for many years to come.

The Need for Consensus

These, then, are the reasons why it appears to me as an inescapable necessity that we should move promptly and resolutely to the achievement of a more workable consensus behind our policy towards the

Soviet Union to take the place of the resounding disagreements that affect, and threaten to paralyze, the formulation and execution of policy in this field today.

I realize, of course, that it is easier to call attention to the need for such a consensus than to chart out the ways in which it could be achieved.

I realize, too, that behind a certain portion of this critical opinion there are commitments of an emotional or political or professional nature which are unlikely to be overcome by appeals to mere reason, and which will have to be confronted, as a political problem, by the responsible political leaders.

But in another portion of this spectrum we have to do with sincerely held and rational opinions, with conclusions drawn from what people believe to be the facts—from the spectrum of facts, or supposed facts, that they now have before them, and I wonder whether, in the case of these people in particular, approaches and devices could not be found— approaches and devices of a basically intellectual nature which would help us importantly, and possibly even decisively, to get on with the solution of this problem. The problem is, after all, a cognitive one; and there is no reason why men of good will should not be able to come to some elements of agreement on the implications for policy of a given body of factual material if they can be brought to a common acceptance of its validity.

And here there are, as I see it, two requirements. First of all, I would propose that we lay aside completely, at least for the moment and for purposes of this exercise I have in mind, the whole question of the military relationship and all the arguments about who could conceivably do what to whom if their intentions were of the nastiest; and that we elevate our vision, at least for the time being, to the question of the real nature and situation of the particular foreign power we are dealing with.

And then, starting with that resolution, I can see in my mind's eye a series of private gatherings in which would be included not only high-level policy-makers of the moment but leading figures of this opposition, as well as possibly a few of the others of us who are interested in Russian affairs—gatherings where we would come together not primarily to discuss matters among ourselves—not to air our prejudices and convictions on the basis of our present knowledge and our present ignorance, but where we would all listen humbly to what could be told to us by the most experienced and knowledgeable people who could be found in the respective fields—I avoid the word "expert" because it implies something more narrow than what I have in mind.

Reeducation in the Realities

What I am thinking of, in other words, is a certain process of reeducation in the realities of Soviet power and leadership—a common effort on the part of all of us who have been prominently involved in this debate—a process in which we would check our existing views at the door, together with our hats, and would listen and ask questions and try to get a new view of the facts before we drew conclusions. I suspect that in an experience of this nature, designed not to promote the clash of old views but to make possible the common development of new, more realistic and more up-to-date ones, we would come closer than in any other way to the composing of our differences.

And there is room for this, I assure you, because no more in the Soviet Union than anywhere else have things been standing still. There are available to us today masses of new factual material on conditions in the Soviet Union—material which, given the rather low state of Soviet studies in our country, has scarcely been digested by the scholars, much less by the policy-makers, the critics and the old-timers in this field of expertise. And in this latter category I include myself. I am much aware that it is exactly 50 years ago that I entered on my own career as a so-called Russian expert, and I think that because of this long preoccupation with the subject—not despite it, mark you, but precisely because of it—it is time that my ideas, too, were taken thoroughly apart and put together again with relation, this time, to the present scene, and not to all the memories I cherish, and all the anecdotes I have been accustomed to telling, about the earlier years.

Such seminars would not, I think, serve their purpose unless they were the product of very high-level initiative and enthusiasm within the administration. But if that initiative and enthusiasm were there, the institutional facilities to organize and accommodate them would not be hard to find.

That is the burden of the song I have come to sing. I am suggesting that the angry controversies over policy toward Russia that are now marring our public debates and threatening the success of any and all

American policies toward that country are not to be solved within the terms of the argument as it is now being conducted—that will come only in a common act of humility—only in the confession that none of us knows too much about what we are talking about—only in the willingness to stop at this point and to learn a little more before we shout each other down. Only in this act of humility will we find the way to a future of Soviet-American relations that offers hope rather than horror.

5. Basic Soviet Institutions Have Not Changed

Richard Pipes

Kennan's Washington speech (see selection 4) was reprinted in its entirety in the March 1978 Encounter. *Writing in the same publication, Professor Richard Pipes—who, like Kennan, is a distinguished scholar of Russian affairs—took issue with Kennan's assertions of far-reaching changes in the Soviet power structure which would justify equally far-reaching changes in the Western defense posture.*

Richard Pipes is Professor of History at Harvard University and was Director of its Russian Research Center. Among his books are The Formation of the Soviet Union, Russia Under the Old Regime, *and* Soviet Strategy in Europe. *He was a member of the famous "Team B" which in 1977 produced an appraisal of the Soviet military posture that was sharply at variance with the "Team A" evaluation of the Washington "intelligence community."*

Reprinted by permission from *Encounter*, April 1978; the article appeared there under the title "Mr. X Revises."

GEORGE KENNAN ADVANCES FOUR related propositions .

1) Since Stalin's death, the Soviet Union has undergone changes of great magnitude, and, although it still retains certain traditional features, including an "authoritarian" system of government, the fact of it being directed by a "moderate" man, "confidently regarded by all who know him as a man of peace" creates conditions favourable to a steady improvement of American-Soviet relations.

2) A mischievous but very influential "Right" opposition in the United States, composed of "military enthusiasts," ignores these changes, and, obsessed with an alleged Soviet military threat, "harasses" those in and out of government who seek to broaden the area of collaboration between the two countries.

3) This "harassment" imperils the evolution of peaceful relations with the Soviet Union, and may, in the end, compel the latter to "look for alternatives other than those of good relations with the United States."

4) The time is opportune for representatives of the two opposing schools of thought on American-Soviet relations to sit down together and work out a "consensus."

I appreciate Mr. Kennan's deeply felt concern. I admire his intelligence and knowledge: unlike many of his persuasion who aggressively flaunt their ignorance of Russian history as a complicating and irrelevant factor, he has read deeply in it. For these reasons I hesitate to take issue with him. I nevertheless do so because I believe all of his propositions, except the last one, to be wrong in the logical as well as political meanings of the word.

Change, Yes, But How Deep?

The Soviet Union has indisputably "changed" since Stalin's death—is there a country in the world that has remained static during the past quarter of a century? But to an historian and political scientist the word "change" conveys something more than mere fluctuations in the political climate, external appearance, and even direction of national policy. It involves, first and foremost, transformations in the basic *institutions* of state and society. In answer to the question: "Has a given state and society changed?" one will want to know what, if anything, of significance has happened to affect the relationship of the government to the country's citizenry and resources—to alter the procedures by means of which government personnel is selected, state policies are determined, and economic wealth is produced and disposed of.

In the case of the Soviet Union, meaningful change would require the introduction of some, even modest, procedures by means of which the population could influence the selection of the Communist Party's directing personnel and their conduct of national affairs. It would provide ordinary citizens with devices to bring to account state officials (including those of the security services) guilty of abusing their authority. It would entail some relaxation of the state's monopoly on the country's economic resources, as expressed in the expansion of the peasantry's land allotments (e.g., to the extent that this is practiced in Poland) and in the granting to industrial labour of the right lawfully to strive for higher wages and better working conditions. Any innovations of this nature would constitute "change" in a sense in which the term has meaning for the historian and political scientist. A package of them would indeed attest to a profound internal transformation of the Soviet system, a new Soviet Russia in the making.

I submit that, unfortunately, no such innovations have occurred. In 1978, the central institutions of the Soviet state remain what they were in Stalin's day, and, for that matter, they are not all that different from the ones Lenin had created in 1917-18, when he gave shape to Communist Russia.

That state is *still* run by a body of men whom no one has ever elected to office and who perpetuate themselves by the device of cooptation. Their power remains absolute, subject neither to constitutional restraints nor to control by popular representatives (in any sense that does not make mockery of these concepts). Neither the state nor its officials can be held accountable for abuses. There exist no restraints on the power of the security services *vis-à-vis* ordinary citizens. The self-appointed élite still controls virtually all of the productive wealth of the country, investing it and disposing of it at will. It continues to be the country's sole employer, and, as such, it is still in a position to render any citizen unemployed and unemployable. The peasants still do not own their land or its produce (save for what they grow on their minuscule private plots). Workmen still cannot strike.

This being the case, it seems entirely inappropriate to speak of "changes" of any magnitude having occurred in the Soviet Union since 1953. The critical fact is not that, in contrast to the 1930s and 1940s, the Soviet Union of the 1970s is directed by a man of moderation and peaceful intent (a questionable proposition at best, but let it stand here for argument's sake). The critical fact is precisely the one that Mr. Kennan disposes of in one casual sentence, namely that the Soviet Union remains an "authoritarian" régime, and that it is such in the very broadest sense of the term.

Mr. Brezhnev is mortal. As Russia is now constituted, there exist no guarantees whatever that his successor, for the selection of whom there are no established procedures, will not turn out to be a man with a very different temperament and predilections. And this man will have at his disposal the whole machinery of internal repression and external aggression which Stalin had left behind at his death—if anything, larger in size and technically vastly improved. Surely we cannot be asked completely to reorient our foreign policy and mortgage our national security to the vagaries of succession in the Soviet Union, given that the underlying institutions of that country remain in all essential respects as they had been under what Mr. Kennan calls Stalin's "ruthless and far-reaching despotism."

Pre-Revolutionary Russia

I am surprised that Mr. Kennan should equate present-day Soviet "authoritarianism" with that of pre-Revolutionary Russia. I happen strongly to believe that the roots of the Soviet régime reach deep into Russian history, especially that of the pre-Petrine era. Nevertheless, I do not see how one can ignore the profound differences between pre-1917 and post-1917 Russian "authoritarianism."

Pre-1917 Russia was a constitutional monarchy with a parliament (a very imperfect one, to be sure) and an independent judiciary. In that Russia the peasant owned the land he tilled as well as the produce which he extracted from it; and the worker was legally entitled to organise and to strike. Imperial Russia in the last sixty years of its existence had in fact undergone such fundamental institutional changes as I have specified above, inasmuch as in the course of that period it had evolved from a serf-owning society ruled by an unlimited autocrat and without a separate judiciary into a quasi-parliamentary constitutional state in which there no longer was serfdom but there were irremovable judges. No comparable evolution has occurred in the Soviet Union during the past sixty years. Such changes as are visible there affect only the political climate: and these are no more trustworthy guidelines for the future than the often dramatic changes that in Imperial Russia had accompanied the succession from one monarch to another, say from Paul I to Alexander I, or from Alexander I to Nicholas I. In taking the death of Stalin as his benchmark for measuring progress, Mr. Kennan is choosing the date most favourable to his case.

Suppose, however, that instead of comparing today's Russia with that of twenty-five years ago, he compared it with that of fifty years ago, when the New Economic Policy was at its height. In every respect Soviet Russia of that time was freer and more conciliatory in its foreign policy than it had been immediately before or than it is today. The basic institutions of the state, however, had not changed since the period of War Communism; and a year or two later Stalin showed the world how quickly policies can be reversed when the mechanism of control remains intact. Incidentally, most of the arguments advanced by Mr. Kennan about the evolving nature of the Soviet régime were first articulated by Russian émigrés in the 1920s, following the introduction of NEP. If Mr. Kennan were to reread the writings of the 1920s by Ekaterina Kuskova, Paul Miliukov, and other proponents of the thesis of the Soviet "Thermidor," and then reflect on their demonstrated fallacy, he might feel less confident of his own predictions.

Those of us who insist on looking at the underlying institutions and structures see none of the profound changes which Mr. Kennan places at the base of his policy recommendations. And for this reason we are troubled by what we perceive to be a relentless growth of Soviet military capabilities, far beyond what seem to us the country's legitimate defence needs. I believe that the facts of this military expansion are not generally in dispute. The disagreement revolves around two corollary questions:

1) What are the reasons behind it—is it self-generated or is it a reaction to American initiatives?

2) What are its implications—does it or does it not pose a serious threat to US and Western security?

I can see legitimate arguments being made on both sides of the debate. I cannot concede, however, that those who take the position that the Soviet military effort is self-generated and threatening are men of the "Right" and "military enthusiasts." There is nothing "Right" about concern with an effective defence. In 1938-39 it was the liberal President of the United States who was pressing, against conservative opposition, for defence appropriations. Today, the leading Russian dissidents, among them Andrei Sakharov, the Nobel Laureate for Peace, men who have given proof of their dedication to liberal and democratic values not only in words but by risking their careers and even lives, warn the West of the pitfalls of "*détente*" and military weakness. And, of course, no one is more vociferous on behalf of a strong Western military stance than the government of the People's Republic of China, which can be labelled "Right" only at the risk of depriving this word of any meaning. As for calling a "military enthusiast" a person who worries about another party's military threat, it strikes me as very perverse: one could just as well call Jeremiah a "doomsday enthusiast."

Military Facts Must Be Faced

Mr. Kennan has no patience with the complexities of the military balance. He confesses to an inability even to understand those who occupy themselves with what he calls "letters and numbers of various weapons systems," "their reputed capabilities," and their "interactions . . . in situations of actual hostility." The statement renders me speechless. Unless Mr. Kennan were to profess pacifism and on principle refuse to respond to force with force—a cause he does not seem to advocate—then how can he urge that we ignore instruments of destruction targeted on our cities, industries, and military establishment? And how does he reconcile his perception of the Soviet leadership as rational with the indisputable fact that it pays enormous attention to and expends vast sums of money on matters which he considers irrational and even irrelevant?

If Mr. Kennan desires a consensus on these questions he simply must start taking seriously the views of those who are concerned with Soviet weapons' developments and see in them indicators of Soviet intentions.

In the past several years, a number of specialists have raised questions about the dominant United States strategic doctrine (which Mr. Kennan seems to share in an extreme formulation) that there can be no victor in nuclear war and hence that the whole issue of "nuclear superiority" is meaningless. Mr. Paul Nitze, an accomplished expert in these matters, has argued at length the possibility of the present US second (retaliatory) strike capability being neutralised by Soviet advances in weaponry. Mr. T. K. Jones has shown, in part experimentally, that Soviet civil defence measures are able greatly to limit Soviet human and material losses in the event of a nuclear war. Mr. Edward Luttwak has analysed the pitfalls of the SALT process. I myself have called attention to the war-fighting and war-winning elements in Soviet nuclear doctrine.

Let me assure Mr. Kennan that these arguments have not found a response so far. Those who share his views have rather preferred to ignore them. The most common reaction to those who address themselves to the realities of the military threat is to raise questions about their putative motives and even sanity. Thus, for instance, Professor George Kistiakowsky in a recent article saw fit collectively to describe all who happen to hold views on strategic matters different from his own as "paranoiacs."

It is for this reason that feelings have grown so intense and a climate of opinion has been created which makes it nearly impossible to arrive at a rational consensus on defence policy. Mr. Kennan is too much of a gentleman to scorn, let alone abuse those with whom he disagrees. And yet even his remarks reveal an ill-concealed impatience with those of his compatriots who for cogently stated reasons occupy themselves with the strategic balance. If he took them and their arguments half seriously he would be bound to conclude that what they are doing is not "harassment" of the administration, but the exercise of their citizen's duty to speak up when they believe the country to be pursuing a dangerous course. I do not suppose that Mr. Kennan would say of the opponents of America's involvement in Vietnam that they "harassed" the Nixon administration and bewail the fact that they had virtually compelled the United States to withdraw from there. And yet these opponents of the then US policy often engaged in physical violence, whereas critics of America's current defence policy confine themselves to argument. Apparently, "harassment," too, is in the eye of the beholder.

Weighing the West's Response

There is no evidence either in past Soviet behaviour or in current Soviet literature to indicate that an effective American and NATO response to its military initiatives would lead the Soviet Union to adopt a more aggressive foreign policy. Admittedly, anyone who has dealings with Soviet diplomats of both the official and unofficial varieties is familiar with "confidential" warnings to this effect; but I find it difficult to believe that a person of Mr. Kennan's experience in these matters could be taken in by such transparent tactics of influencing American and European public opinion.

But then I also do not share Mr. Kennan's view of current Soviet foreign policy as conservative and pacific. I cannot understand how these terms can be applied to a government which under Mr. Brezhnev's leadership has invaded Czechoslovakia, threatened to invade China and Romania, conspired twice with Egypt and Syria to attack Israel, assisted North Viet Nam to conquer South Viet Nam and a pro-Soviet government to seize Angola, and today feeds the flames of war between Somalia and Ethiopia.

While the perils of a strong American and European defence stance on international relations are questionable, those of a weak one appear to me very real. Perhaps the worst of these, from a political point of view, is the possibility that it may drive the Chinese to seek a *rapprochement* with the Soviet Union. The Chinese leadership makes no secret of what it thinks of Soviet capabilities and intentions, and how worried it is about what it perceives to be the unwillingness of the West to match them. Should it conclude that the United States is not a reliable ally against the Soviet striving for "hegemony," then the option of a *rapprochement* with the USSR will almost certainly come to the fore in China and find supporters there.

I consider this threat to be much more genuine than Russia's possible abandonment of *détente,* and far more dangerous in its implications. There is no historic evidence to suggest that the Soviet government responds to toughness with toughness, and to conciliation with conciliation. The only time in its history that the Soviet Union may be said to have appeased another power was in 1939-41 in its relations with Hitler. I do not recall it reciprocating President Roosevelt's conciliatory policies in the latter stages of World War II.

All these are complicated and grave issues. A meeting of minds is clearly in order: a consensus may or may not emerge from it, but at least the two schools of thought, presently snarling at one another, will learn better to understand, and, we hope to respect each other's point of view.

But this surely calls for a genuine dialogue. The rules of the discourse cannot be drawn up as Mr. Kennan proposes, namely by agreeing "to lay aside completely [!], at least for the moment and for pur-

poses of this exercise, the whole question of the military relationship"
in order to concentrate on the "real nature and situation" in the Soviet
Union.

A debate between two parties, one of which regards the military
relationship as crucial to the understanding of the "real nature and
situation" of the Soviet Union, cannot begin by placing this topic out
of bounds. If those who share my views are to be drawn into a discussion
of present-day Soviet society and its evolution, then those who share
Mr. Kennan's opinions will have to suffer through instruction about
the strategic balance and the relationship between the Soviet military
drive and Soviet intentions.

6. The Banality of Evil

Michael Novak

✿ ✿ ✿ ✿ ✿ ✿ ✿ ✿ ✿ ✿ ✿ ✿ ✿ ✿ ✿ ✿

Ambassador Kennan has voiced distress that the arguments in his 1947 "X" article, which had been intended for "naive, over-trusting, overidealistic" persons of the left, are now used against him "from the opposite end of the spectrum." To this, Professor Novak responds that many of those who take issue with Kennan's current views are actually men of the moderate left. He fails to see why the fact that the current leaders of the Kremlin are a gerontocracy should inspire confidence; and he, like Richard Pipes, believes that it is quite possible to have a rational debate on Soviet and American defense policies—but charges Kennan with avoiding such a debate.

A syndicated columnist, Michael Novak is also Ledden-Watson Professor of Religious Studies at Syracuse University. He is the author of Politics: Realism and Imagination *and* The Rise of the Unmeltable Ethnics.

✿ ✿ ✿ ✿ ✿ ✿ ✿ ✿ ✿ ✿ ✿ ✿ ✿ ✿ ✿ ✿

Reprinted by permission from *The Washington Star*, December 29, 1977; the article appeared there under the title "George X. Kennan versus George Y. Kennan."

JUST 30 YEARS AGO, in 1947, a certain "Mr. X" wrote a paper about the Soviets for "Foreign Affairs" which became a landmark in the theory of "containment." Today, Mr. X, who was revealed to be George F. Kennan, has begun to write so differently about Soviet-American affairs that his work seems written by someone else altogether—as if by some "Mr. Y."

The new Mr. Kennan seems to think that the main enemy of the United States is within. The enemy is those Americans who disagree with his new optimism about the Soviets.

In a paper given before the Council on Foreign Relations on November 22, 1977, Mr. Kennan says that 30 years ago he opposed "left-wing deviationists," because they had a "naive, overtrusting, idealistic view" of Russia. Mostly these were New York intellectuals; many were Jews. Today, Mr. Kennan says his opposition comes from "the opposite end of the political spectrum," the far right. But, in fact, Mr. Kennan's present opposition comes not from the right but from the left, from liberal Democrats, even social democrats, like Senators Henry M. Jackson and Daniel Patrick Moynihan; the Social Democrats, U.S.A.; several contributors to "Commentary" magazine, and many distinguished liberal intellectuals. Many, as he explicitly suggests, are Jews. Far from representing "the opposite end of the political spectrum," Mr. Kennan's present critics are liberals who do not see in actual Soviet behavior today the sweetness Kennan sees.

The new Mr. Kennan dwells on "the magnitude of the changes that have occurred" in the Soviet Union during the last 30 years. He says "there is very little to be seen today of the terror that prevailed in Stalin's time; and the regime is headed by a moderate, in fact conservative, man . . . a man of the middle . . . a man of peace. . . ." He is not describing Pope John XXIII, nor Adlai Stevenson, nor Winston Churchill—he means Leonid Brezhnev.

Mr. Kennan writes of the Soviet leaders as if they were less mature than we, in need of tender reassurance. He describes them as "victims," victims of the "ideology on which they were reared . . . a group of quite ordinary men . . . highly conservative men, perhaps the most conservative ruling group to be found anywhere in the world." He sees them as "markedly advanced in age, approaching the end of their tenure, and given to everything else but rash adventure." He sees in the Soviet leaders "men more seriously concerned to preserve the limits of their political power . . . than to expand those limits—men whose motivation is essentially defensive and whose attention is riveted primarily to unsolved problems of economic development . . . men who suffer greatly under the financial burden . . . of (their) present bloated arsenals. . . ." Genial Fabians, nice men.

Mr. Kennan does not describe Soviet leaders as Solzhenitsyn does. He does not cite the corrupting practises they daily enforce. The "bloated arsenals" he speaks of are of their own making, hard evidence of where they put their money. Mr. Kennan believes that his American opponents think the Soviet leaders are a "terrible and forbidding group of men—monsters of sorts, really, because lacking in all elements of common humanity."

But Mr. Kennan is wrong. Those of us who oppose him remember full well Hannah Arendt's insight into the "banality of evil." The enemies of liberty in this world are not monsters but quite ordinary men, with nieces and nephews and beloved daughters, with a fondness for special dishes and a delight in jokes—men like you or me.

One's enemies are by no means monsters in appearance. One watches, not the state of their psyches, but their chosen courses of action.

Mr. Kennan finds a discussion of the actual weapons systems financed by Soviet leaders beyond his comprehension; it makes him, he admits, dizzy. He would rather not get the "military mathematics" straight—too many variables, complexities, and uncertainties for him.

But the Soviets are building this, and that, and the other; and each system they build has a precise operational range and function. Perhaps Mr. Kennan cannot square what the Soviets are actually doing with his own benign interpretation of their psychology.

Furthermore, if Mr. Kennan thinks the Soviet leaders are pining for surcease from military burdens, he should consider Jimmy Carter, the Rockefellers, and himself. There is far less evidence of change in Soviet imperial ambition between 1947 and 1977 than of change in American resolve.

Military expenditures do not mean that the Soviets desire war. Military power enables them to achieve by negotiation what they would have to acquire otherwise through war. Superior military might makes war unnecessary. Consider the surrenders Mr. Kennan now urges the United States to make. Is not the source of these surrenders our elite's own loss of heart?

Mr. Kennan recognizes implicitly that the U.S. is no longer in a position to "contain" an expanding Soviet imperial power. The best we can hope is "accommodation." In 1947, Mr. X was bold and assertive. In 1977, Mr. Y is weary, timid, and ready to yield. When the other party holds the aces, gentlemen decline tests of strength. They salvage their dignity by pleading, as Mr. Kennan now does, for "humility," by recanting their bolder youth, and by discovering that their adversaries are nice men, after all. The alchemy of weakness has changed "Mr. X" into "Mr. Y."

7. Is Brezhnev a Man of Peace?

Seymour Weiss

Ambassador Seymour Weiss spent thirty of his thirty-three years of government service as a specialist in national security affairs, holding positions of increasing importance in the White House and the Department of State; these culminated in his directorship of the Bureau of Political-Military Affairs. He is currently president of a Washington consulting firm and adjunct professor of the Center for Advanced International Studies of Miami University. In his government positions he was associated with NATO planning, the defense of Berlin, the Cuban Missile Crisis, SALT I, and related matters.

FOR THOSE OF US WHO LABORED at formulating a sensible post-World War II national security policy, the views of George Kennan were received with respectful attention. Mr. Kennan, it will be recalled, was the mysterious "Mr. X" who in 1947 analyzed Soviet policy objectives in the prestigious magazine Foreign Affairs.

Mr. X saw those objectives, derived as they were from Russian ideology and culture, as based upon an "innate antagonism between capitalism and socialism" accompanied by an "infallible" belief in the eventual triumph of the latter. To resist the Soviet impulse toward expansion, Mr. X proposed what came to be known as the "containment policy," designed to oppose the Russians wherever they tried to encroach "upon the interests of a peaceful and stable world."

When it became known that Mr. X was George Kennan, director of the State Department's policy planning staff, his views were accorded wide attention. Much of early U.S. postwar policy, including the Marshall Plan and the North Atlantic Treaty Organization, appeared as corollaries to Mr. Kennan's concept of the need to contain the Soviet threat.

So it is with special interest that one learns that Mr. Kennan has reassessed the nature of U.S.-Soviet relations in a recent presentation to the Council on Foreign Relations. This reassessment stands in striking contrast to his earlier views.

In place of the Stalinist mode, Mr. Kennan tells us the Soviet Union is today ruled by "a man confidently regarded by all who know him as a man of peace." In place of containment, Mr. Kennan now sees "improvement in the objective possibilities for a better Soviet-American relationship" where there are areas in which "interests largely coincide and limited collaboration is possible."

As Mr. Kennan sees it, the ability to capitalize upon this new-found opportunity is endangered by those who concern themselves unduly with the military (and especially the nuclear-military) relationship between the Soviet Union and the United States. Mr. Kennan urges that there be a new dialog within the U.S. involving a "process of reeducation in the realities of Soviet power and leadership."

Regrettably, Mr. Kennan does not suggest the bounds of a new relationship with the Soviets.

But does he see a cooperative relationship on issues central to U.S. security interests or is cooperation likely to be limited to more marginal, more cosmetic issues? Mr. Kennan does not supply the answer though he perhaps offers a hint in asserting that the present leadership of the U.S.S.R. is perhaps "the most conservative ruling group to be found anywhere in the world . . . given to anything but rash adventure."

One wonders whether Mr. Kennan is referring to the leadership that is presently supporting a war on the continent of Africa with significant numbers of Soviet military advisers and through massive supply of arms to Communist mercenaries. Or the leadership that in 1973 threatened unilateral military intervention in the Middle East and that today stimulates Arab resistance to efforts to bring peace to the area. Or the leadership that marched into Czechoslovakia.

Mr. Kennan's description of this leadership stands in sharp contrast to his views expressed at a meeting of longtime Soviet experts held in 1975. At that time Mr. Kennan described the regime as having "more blood on its hands than any regime in the world today"; a regime which had been "driving out or killing the more intelligent" and sensitive of the Russians, leaving what he described as "a pretty primitive mass of people."

One is left confused by Mr. Kennan's views of Soviet leadership and objectives and the degree to which "cooperation" can be attained without sacrifice of fundamental U.S. interests and values. Mr. Kennan implies, for example, that an agreement on strategic arms is one area for an improved relationship with the Soviets. The alternative, Mr. Kennan tells us, is an "unlimited arms race."

Does he believe such a race has been taking place? What percentage of our own defense budget does he believe we have been spending on strategic nuclear arms? (In fact, it is about 10%.) And even without a SALT agreement, wouldn't there be political, economic and military restraints on a "race totally out of control"?

Mr. Kennan warns us that "the penalties of failure" to reach an agreement on SALT "are too serious" to be permitted. Any agreement? Could not a conceptually faulty agreement worsen rather than ameliorate suspicions and uncertainties? Mr. Kennan does not say, though he hints that it may not matter much since both sides, he asserts, have excessive nuclear overkill. Nor does he take account of the effect of the nuclear balance on our alliances.

Even if Mr. Kennan is correct, as I believe he is, that the Soviet Union seeks no war with us, how genuinely revealing is this insight? Historically, have wars normally occurred because one nation consciously sought war? Or, is the likelihood of war more a function of the pursuit by nations of opposed national objectives?

In his 1947 article Mr. Kennan said: ''It must invariably be assumed in Moscow that the aims of the capitalist world are antagonistic to the Soviet regime and, therefore, to the interests of the peoples it controls. If the Soviet government occasionally sets its signature to documents which would indicate the contrary, this is to be regarded as a tactical maneuver permissible in dealing with the enemy (who is without honor) and should be taken in the spirit of *caveat emptor.''*

If Mr. Kennan now means to abandon or significantly modify this past assessment, much more in the way of substantive clarification and elaboration of his present position is required.

PART TWO

While almost all the points in the developing controversy over Mr. Kennan's thinking were foreshadowed in Part One, they find more systematic development in Part Two, which centers on Kennan's latest book, *The Cloud of Danger*. It is a wide-ranging book, from which we excerpt only the salient portions dealing with East-West security matters.

Two critics—one a distinguished academic and former high government official, the other a civilian expert on military strategy—help to bring into high relief the aspects of Kennan's thinking that are most novel and controversial. Here the basic issue appears to be more clearly joined.

8. The Cloud of Danger

George F. Kennan

☆ ☆ ☆ ☆ ☆ ☆ ☆ ☆ ☆ ☆ ☆ ☆ ☆ ☆ ☆ ☆

In 1977, Ambassador Kennan distilled fragments of his thinking into "something resembling a grand design of American foreign policy." The result was The Cloud of Danger: Current Realities of American Foreign Policy. *In this 234-page book, Mr. Kennan addresses a wide range of regional and functional issues confronting the United States.*

In two chapters devoted to the Soviet Union and one to Soviet-American relations, Kennan repeats but refines the views he expressed in his Encounter *interview (see selection 2).*

To give the reader a taste of The Cloud of Danger, *five brief, non-continuous sections —"The Military-Industrial Complex," "Soviet Intentions," "Soviets and World Domination," "Soviet Leadership," and "The Military Danger" —are printed below.*

☆ ☆ ☆ ☆ ☆ ☆ ☆ ☆ ☆ ☆ ☆ ☆ ☆ ☆ ☆ ☆

The Military-Industrial Complex

A SECOND PHENOMENON of American life which has to be borne in mind when one thinks about this country's situation from the standpoint of the conduct of foreign affairs is the military-industrial complex. By this I mean, of course, the weight of military purchasing in our economy, the role of the Pentagon as a factor in our industrial life, and the effect of all this on our society.

The general outlines of this phenomenon are well known. Defense spending is now passing the one-hundred-billion-dollar mark, with the purchases of military hardware running well over $30 billion per annum, to which should be added, at least for purposes of this discussion, some $10 billion more for arms aid and sales to other countries.* This makes the Pentagon clearly the greatest purchaser in the United States, absorbing about 6 percent of the total national output of goods and services.

Now all this has several effects worth noting:

First of all, there is the inflationary effect. Whether the extensive purchasing of services and materials to be used for military purposes is or is not *in itself* inflationary is something about which economists, I gather, can and do disagree. (It certainly places in circulation enormous quantities of money in return for goods and services that are largely lost to the normal productive economy of the country.) But there could be no disagreement, I think, over the fact that it has strongly inflationary side-effects. No one who has had occasion to observe at first hand the workings of the armed services could fail to observe the lavish way in which money is used, as compared with functions that are obliged to meet the normal competition of private life. And it would be hard to believe that those who control military purchasing from the Pentagon end are generally able to exercise the same restraining pressure on the prices of what they buy as are private companies which have to meet the test of the balance sheet. Indeed, there are a number of reasons, including time pressures and the noncompetitive nature of many of the items purchased, why they would find it hard to do this even with the best of will and the sternest standards of integrity. (Having

---

*The involvement of the Pentagon with both military aid programs and arms sales to foreign governments is so extensive, and the effects of these programs are so similar to those of purchases for the U.S. forces, that they constitute an essential part of the problem here under discussion.

written this, I note the following passage from an article [*New York Times*, December 14, 1976] by Mr. Seymour Melman, Professor of Industrial Engineering at Columbia University:

Unlike civilian firms that traditionally minimize production costs to maximize profits, firms in the Pentagon's economy *maximize* all costs and the offsetting subsidies. These translate into rising prices.

The United States military economy is an inflation machine. From top to bottom cost and price increases are encouraged and rewarded; these practices are carried into and infect civilian parts of firms serving the Pentagon, and other enterprises. The classic processes of offsetting cost increases by mechanization and other efficiency-promoting measures are neglected. Higher costs are added to prices.)

Regardless of the extent to which the Pentagon may have been a contributor to the inflation, it has obviously been a major victim of it. The evidences of this are striking, and alarming. It is estimated that replacement costs of major items of equipment for the armed services, particularly aircraft and naval vessels, are now running three to five times higher than those of the items they are designed to replace, although many of the latter have been in use only a few years. The reduction in the size of various forces which was expected to take place, and to a limited extent did take place, with the termination of the Vietnam War, has not been attended by any corresponding reduction in military costs; on the contrary, it is now costing more, in a number of instances, to maintain the reduced forces than it did to maintain the larger ones of the pre-Vietnam and Vietnam periods.

All this testifies, in a general way, to the inflationary effects of great military spending; but it testifies also to a secondary fact of great importance, often missed in the discussion of problems of military competition with the Soviet Union: namely, that we are steadily pricing ourselves out of the running. Even if it were true that we were rapidly being overtaken and left at a disadvantage by the rate of development of the Russian armed forces (and about this I shall have something to say at a different point in this discussion), we ought to recognize that the reason for this, if carefully examined, would turn out to lie less in the pace and dimensions of the Soviet effort than in the wildly increasing expensiveness of our own. Considering the rate at which the costs of national defense are now being permitted to rise in this country, we can hardly expect to keep up in such a competition except at an enormous, steadily increasing, and finally almost prohibitive cost to our economy as a whole. Yet one sees little recognition of this in the public and congressional discussions of the defense budget. If the protagonists of heavy military spending really wished to find the shortest path to the correction of what they see as a growing disbalance to our disfavor in the relative strength of Soviet and American forces, they would do well to give more attention to our own inflation, and especially to the effects of that inflation on the military budget, and less to the effort to convince the rest of us of the menacing intentions and fearful strength of our Soviet opponents.

But there is another effect of the military-industrial complex, beyond the inflationary one, that deserves our notice. Such massive military spending leads to a curious double standard in the evaluation and use of money, as between those involved in this military spending and all the rest of us. It means that there is a group of people in Washington who, together with their counterparts in industry, are accustomed to thinking of millions of dollars in much the same way the rest of us think of thousands. One time, when I was at sea on one of our naval vessels and watching several forms of target practice, I was struck by the realization that each one of a certain class of missiles that were being fired off with great abandon (and not recovered) had cost more than my entire Pennsylvania farm, itself the product of generations of back-breaking work. Yet I am sure that this thought never entered the heads of the officers who were in charge of the target practice. And why should it? There were plenty more of these missiles where their stock had come from. No one asked about costs. No one had seriously asked about them when the missiles were originally ordered. In the view of those who did the purchasing, these costs were chicken feed.

Now I am not saying that this sort of thing could be avoided. The activities of the military in peacetime consist, after all, of playing with a great many expensive toys; and it is hard to find criteria of financial prudence applicable to the process of playing with toys. But I *am* saying that it leads, unavoidably, to a double standard in the way people think about money. And this double standard makes it hard to find valid means of comparison between military needs and those of the civilian economy. When military spending grows to such vast dimensions, and proceeds at such vast and inflated expense, it tends to cut loose from all normal considerations of relative usefulness as compared with other functions of our governmental and economic life and to begin to lead a life of its own in a never-never world where three zeros are added, as though it were the most natural thing in the world, to every normal figure, where millions become for their manipulators what thousands are to the rest of us. It becomes a question, then, how the billion-dollar economy is to be controlled, indeed whether it can be controlled at all, by those whose concepts are formed in a whole different stratum of monetary values.

To this we must add the reflection that this vast flow of military spending comes to constitute a vested interest on the part of all those who participate in it and benefit from it. This includes not just the industrialists who get the money, and the Pentagon purchasers who get the hardware and services, but also all those who benefit from the arrangement in other ways: not only the uniformed personnel of the armed services but those who serve the Pentagon directly as civilian workers, and beyond them the many more who, as workers in defense plants or in other capacities, share in the spin-off from these vast expenditures. These latter alone are estimated to number over two million. All of these people come, of course, to have a stake in the perpetuation of high defense spending. And since the workers in defense industry, in particular, tend to live in compact blocs in single congressional districts, and to be associated with powerful unions, their political punch is powerful. The individual congressman finds himself exposed to pressures from three sides: from the industrialists, who want the orders and the money; from the military, who want the hardware and the services; and from the defense workers and their unions, who want the defense-connected jobs. This is a powerful combination—so powerful, in fact, that it sometimes compels the congressman himself to become in effect a shareholder in the huge vested interest which it all represents.

What this means is that our practice (now a habit) of permitting the Pentagon to put out more than a hundred billion dollars each year for what are ostensibly the requirements of national defense has become something much more than a feature of defense policy—it has become a species of national-economic addiction—a habit which we could not easily or rapidly break, in fact, in the course of anything less than several years, even if the entire external justification for it were to disappear—even if the Soviet Union were to sink tomorrow, with all its armies and missiles, to the bottom of the ocean.

I am not trying to say, here, that there is not, along with these internal compulsions, a serious measure of justification for such expenditures arising from the real needs of national defense. But I am saying that these two motivations coexist in the governmental decisions out of which our defense expenditures flow, and that it is very difficult to decide, in any given instance, where one stops and the other begins. Defense spending, in other words, is not just a means to a single end: the assurance of our external security in an uncertain and unstable world; it is also a condition of American society—one which has profound effects on our domestic-political life, and one which constitutes one more limitation on our ability to shape and execute our foreign policies in response to external challenges.

For the designing of one's defense posture—the measures one takes, that is, in the development of armed strength—are not just domestic measures: they are, whether one intends them this way or not, acts of foreign policy. They affect other governments. They influence the policies those other governments pursue. Yet here, in the field of defense preparation and defense spending, we have a set of acts of foreign policy the dimensions and nature of which we cannot determine just on the basis of external necessity alone. To an appreciable extent we are obliged to perform certain actions in this field on the basis of domestic-political necessity, carry us where they will in our external relations. And this is only another way of saying that we are faced here, once again, with a limitation on our freedom to conduct a foreign policy which would be, from the standpoint of its external effects, coherent and consistently purposeful.

Soviet Intentions

On examining these various warnings of heightened Soviet aggressiveness and determination to achieve military superiority, one is struck by certain implicit assumptions that seem to run through them concerning the nature and intentions of the Soviet leadership. These might be summarized as follows:

(a) That the Soviet leadership has not significantly changed since the days of the Cold War and is still primarily inspired by a desire, and intention, to achieve world domination.

(b) That the Soviet leadership views a military showdown with the United States as the inevitable outcome of the ideological and political conflict between the two powers, and looks only for an opportunity to attack the United States and its NATO allies successfully, or to confront them with such overpowering military force that they will "surrender" and place themselves in its power.

(c) That for this reason, the Soviet armed forces serve, in the eyes of the leaders, primarily aggressive rather than defensive purposes.

Supplementing these views there seems to be an assumption on the part of the spokesmen of this thesis, themselves, that the differences of aim and outlook between the Soviet Union and the United States are indeed of such a nature that no peaceful resolution of them is conceivable—that they can be resolved only by war or by the achievement of an unanswerable military superiority by the one party or the other.

I hope to be able, in the following chapter, to treat this question of Soviet intentions at greater length and more adequately. But there are one or two things about these assumptions that ought to be said at this point.

First: When people suggest or imply that there is no significant difference between the Soviet Union we knew at the close of the Stalin era, a quarter of a century ago, and that which we have before us today, this is a sign that those same people have not looked very attentively or deeply at either the composition or the situation of the Soviet regime. Actually, even Stalin, in his final years, seems to have accepted the inevitability, or probability, of an eventual military showdown not because he himself wanted it or thought it necessary from the Soviet standpoint, but rather because he thought the Western powers were determined to push things to that point. But whatever he may then have thought, there is no reason to suppose that the present leadership would see things precisely as he did.

Certainly, if all this could be achieved bloodlessly, without upsetting repercussions at home and without increased responsibilities for the Soviet Union abroad, the leadership of that country would no doubt be pleased—but only within limits—to see such things as abandonment of the Western position in Berlin, a clear Soviet military ascendancy all the way from the Atlantic to the Chinese frontier, and heightened Soviet prestige the world over. Whether they would really like to see a dismantling of American military power in Western Europe is questionable. But that this leadership would wish to see all this achieved by war, even if this could be done with only a relatively moderate amount of military damage to the Soviet Union, is highly doubtful. I must dismiss, as unworthy of serious attention, the suggestion that the

Soviet leaders would be prepared to accept a loss of several tens of millions of the Soviet population in a nuclear encounter if it could thereby expect to establish a military superiority over the United States. The memories and trauma of World War II are far more active in Russia than people in the West seem generally to realize. Wars, particularly ones waged at distance from the center of Russian power and for purposes that did not seem to include the defense of the heartland, have always been politically dangerous in modern times to Russian governments. And there are other, more subjective reasons for such hesitations on the part of the present leadership, which it will be more useful to treat in the next chapter.

But beyond this, the people who profess to see some sort of a military showdown as inevitable, allegedly because the Soviet leaders are determined to have it, seem themselves to be only too ready to accept that same thesis for themselves, as something flowing from the logic of the conflict of aims and ideals between the two countries. This is perhaps the most dangerous of all the elements in their thinking. For competitive military preparations, pursued over a long period of time, conduce insensibly to the assumption that a military conflict so long and intensively prepared for must at some point take place. People tend, then, to forget that perhaps there was nothing in the actual interests and needs of the respective peoples to justify a war in the first place.

Bismarck, in the final years of his active life, had to contend with just this problem in the tendency of the German military leaders, and many senior political officials in his country, to regard a German-Russian war as inevitable just because the elaborate preparations of the military establishments on both sides of the line made it appear so. In vain, he pleaded with people to understand that Germany had no objectives with regard to Russia that were worth the sacrifices of a war—that war would bring disaster to both parties—such disaster that at the end of it people would no longer even remember the relatively trivial bones of contention out of which it had arisen.

And so it is, today. There is no political or ideological difference between the Soviet Union and the United States—nothing which either side would like, or would hope, to achieve at the expense of the other— that would be worth the risks and sacrifices of a military encounter. Given a realistic appreciation of the limitations of great-power imperialism, and particularly of Russian imperialism, in the modern age, it would be cheaper, safer, and less damaging over the long term for either side to yield on any of the points of difference between them rather than to accept the disaster which modern war would spell. This has been repeatedly demonstrated by recent history. It is evident, for example, that in 1916, in the middle of World War I, either side could have accepted the maximum terms of the other side for ending the war and have been better off than it was by continuing the war for another two years. (To observe this is not to make a plea for political surrender. It is merely to urge that we get our thinking straight.)

While there are no doubt individuals in the Soviet hierarchy of power who do not understand this, there is abundant evidence that the Soviet leadership as a whole does. War, consequently, or even the risk of it that would be implied in any all-out effort to achieve military superiority, is not their favored means of achieving such of their objectives as seem to be in conflict with those of the United States. Nor do any of these objectives, insofar as we can observe them—particularly in Eurrasia—seem to be of such a nature as to challenge any vital interest of ours—the only possible exception being Berlin. There appear, however, most unfortunately, to be numbers of Americans to whom none of this is apparent.

It has been noted above that the tendency of the American military mind, when confronted with the argument that the Soviet leaders are perhaps neither determined to do, or even desirous of doing, to us all the dreadful things of which we are now being warned, is to say: ''We cannot make assumptions about Soviet intentions. The evidence is too vague and too complex. We must assume them desirous of doing anything injurious to us which they have the capability of doing.''

Does it never occur to these people, one wonders, that in taking that position they are themselves making a sweeping assumption about Soviet intentions—namely, the most extreme, most pessimistic, least sophisticated, and most improbable assumption they could make—the assumption, namely, that these, their political opponents, lack all the normal attributes of humanity and are motivated by nothing but the most blind and single-minded urge of destruction towards the peoples and substance of the United States and its allies?

This effort at the dehumanization of the opponent—the insistence on seeing him as the embodiment of all evil, unaffected by motives other than the desire to wreak injury upon others—has bedeviled the leaders of American opinion in two world wars. There should be no place for it in the assessment of another great power in peacetime, and particularly not of one with whom our political differences are not such as to require or justify a war for their settlement. Particularly should there be no place for it in an age when war between great nuclear-armed powers has become mortally dangerous to all participants—as well as nonparticipants.

If the United States is to behave, in the face of the problem of Soviet power, in a manner conducive to its own present security and that of future generations, it has no choice but to put this sort of childishness behind it and consent to look at that power soberly and carefully, for what it is, not for what would fit best into the dialectics of theoretical military planning.

To me, the above considerations not only suggest but conclusively demonstrate that the general thesis of a new and heightened danger to this country from recent Soviet military preparations is not supported by the available evidence and has to be rejected as the basis for a useful discussion of the problem now presented to American policy-makers by the phenomenon of Soviet power.

This does not mean that there is no problem at all. It also does not mean that no improvement or strengthening is in order anywhere in the American defense posture. Just as certain adjustments no doubt need to be made in the composition and deployment of American naval strength, so it is entirely possible, even probable, that there is need for changes in the ground force dispositions of NATO in Europe, as is being argued from certain elements on the military side, with a view to reducing their vulnerability to sudden attack, improving their logistical support, and so on. It is perfectly possible that a proper posture for these NATO conventional forces would require further strengthening in one way or another; and the considerations set forth above are not intended as an argument against anything of that sort, where the situation really warrants it. Obviously, the NATO aerial and ground force establishment in Western Europe plays a stabilizing political role; it should not be unilaterally dismantled or seriously weakened; and where strengthening is really needed to assure its suitability to the role it is asked to play, that strengthening should be given.

But there is no reason for persuading oneself that such strengthening, or the strengthening of the strategic nuclear "deterrent," is necessitated by changes in Soviet political and military intentions for which there is no adequate evidence. There is, in fact, the weightiest of reasons for not doing just that; because history has proved that the exaggeration of an adversary's negative attributes, including the evilness of his intentions and the strength he possesses for realizing those supposedly evil intentions, takes on the quality of a self-fulfilling prophecy and tends to promote the arrival of the very dangers it attempts to portray. We have serious enough problems in world affairs today without convincing ourselves of the existence of ones we do not really have.

The Soviets and World Domination

. . . It will be said, of course: yes, but dreams of world domination and a persistent tendency to expansion, as characteristics of Russian outlooks and actions, were not new to Russia in the Communist period; they could be observed for centuries in the conduct of Tsarist statesmen. And, it will further be asked, as the Communist leaders come to conform more closely to the traditional patterns of Russian statesmanship, will not the original ideological motives for aggressive policies simply be replaced, then, by the more traditional ones?

The point is a good one, and not to be answered in a word. In the period of the Grand Duchy of Moscow the intolerant religious orthodoxy on which, in part, the grand dukes based their claim to the legitimacy of their power had global implications. It is also true that in both periods of Tsarist history—Muscovite and Petersburg—the Russian state showed a persistent tendency to what might be called border expansion, extending its power, time after time, to new areas contiguous to the existing frontiers.

The first of these phenomena had serious significance only in the Muscovite period. It was comparable to the ideological orthodoxy of the Soviet period, but was equally remote from any possibility of realization. For this reason it was, like its later-day Marxist counterpart, not very important as a guide to action.

The second of the two phenomena—the tendency to border expansion—affected both Muscovite and Petersburg statesmanship, and has indeed manifested itself in the Soviet period as well. (Stalin was highly affected by it.) It thus poses a more serious question. If it does not play a prominent part in the motivation of Soviet leaders today, this is a product, one must assume, of the force of circumstances rather than of natural inclination.

In the West, Stalin left Russia saddled with so vast a *glacis*—so vast a protective belt—in the form of the satellite area, and this represented in itself so serious a responsibility and in some ways a burden, that there was not only no strong incentive for his successors to expand it (West Berlin being the major exception), but any such effort would have posed considerable danger. On the Asiatic border, the stalemate in Korea (after 1952) and the anxious vigilance of the Chinese made further expansion impossible except at the risk of a major war. This left only three border regions of any significance: Afghanistan, where, for the moment, the situation was not such as to invite or justify expansionist moves on the Russian side; Iran, where again the risks were higher and the possible profit very small; and finally, the Scandinavian North, where the NATO activity and the naval rivalry indeed provided new defensive incentives for an extension of Russian power but where, again, the NATO involvement meant that any attempt to realize such an extension would involve very high risks of major war.

In these circumstances, the traditional Russian tendency to border expansion has found few promising outlets, and except in Asia—little incentive in recent years. It may make itself felt again in the more distant future. For the moment it is not a major component in Soviet motivation. It is, in any case, an impulse which is regional, not universal, in character.

There is one last facet of Soviet policy that will perhaps be cited as evidence of the alleged desire to achieve "world domination." That is the extent to which Moscow has recently involved itself with the resistance movements of Southern Africa and with leftist political factions in other Third World countries.

I am afraid that I am unable to see in this phenomenon anything that is particularly new, anything that falls outside the normal patterns of great-power behavior, anything that proceeds from purely aggressive, as distinct from defensive, motives, or anything reflecting a belief that there is a serious prospect for a major extension of Soviet power through such involvements.

The effort to assist to the seats of power in distant countries factions whose aims seem reasonably compatible with one's own is, as I have already noted, not foreign to the normal practice of great powers, including the United States. Why it should cause such great surprise or alarm when it proceeds from the Soviet Union I fail to understand. The high degree of responsiveness of African resistance leaders to pseudo-Marxist ideas and methods, justifying as these do both heavy

· bloodshed as a means to the attainment of power and the establishment
· of a ruthless dictatorship to assure the maintenance of it, presents a
powerful invitation to Soviet involvement and one which, incidentally,
they can scarcely reject without playing into the hands of the Chinese
critics and rivals. Too often, a failure on the Soviet side to respond to
such appeals for support is to throw the respective factions into the
arms of the Chinese.

In any case, recent Soviet efforts along this line would appear to
have been on a scale hardly comparable to our own, and no greater
than those of the Chinese. The Russians have known no Vietnams in
recent years. They have not even sent their own forces abroad into
other countries (the exception being the Eastern European region which
we, by tacit consent, assigned to their good graces in 1945)—a measure
of restraint which we Americans can scarcely claim for ourselves. And
such efforts as they have made to support factions agreeable to their
concepts and purposes in Third World countries do not strike me as
exceeding, either in nature or in scale, the efforts their Communist
predecessors mounted, without inspiring great alarm in American opinion, in earlier decades.

All in all, then, these apprehensions of a Russian quest for "world
domination," which have been used to justify appeals for a totally
negative, hostile, and militaristic attitude towards the Soviet Union,
have little substance behind them and are not responsive to the real
profile of the problem which the existence of Communist power in
Russia presents for American statesmanship.

Soviet Leadership

. . . If these considerations have any validity, the position of the
Soviet leadership might be summed up somewhat as follows:

This is an aging, highly experienced, and very steady leadership,
itself not given to rash or adventuristic policies. It commands, and is
deeply involved with, a structure of power, and particularly a higher
bureaucracy, that would not easily lend itself to the implementation of
policies of that nature. It faces serious internal problems, which constitute its main preoccupation.

As this leadership looks abroad, it sees more dangers than inviting
opportunities. Its reactions and purposes are therefore much more
defensive than aggressive. It has no desire for any major war, least of

all for a nuclear one. It fears and respects American military power even as it tries to match it, and hopes to avoid a conflict with it. Plotting an attack on Western Europe would be, in the circumstances, the last thing that would come into its head.

The most active external concerns of this leadership relate, today, to the challenge to its position within the world Communist movement now being mounted by the Chinese and others. It will consider itself fortunate if, in the face of this challenge, it succeeds in preserving its pre-eminence within the Communist sector of the world's political spectrum, in avoiding a major war which, as it clearly recognizes, would be the ruin of everyone involved, itself included, and in ending its own days peacefully—its members going down in history as constructive leaders who contributed, much more than Stalin and at least as much as Khrushchev, to the advancement of the glory of the Soviet Union and the cause of world communism.

The Military Danger

Let us, first of all, divest ourselves of the widespread fixation that our differences with the Russians must someday end in war—or that military strength, in any case, must be the ultimate arbiter of them. A war between the two countries is not inevitable. The Soviet leaders themselves, and outstandingly Brezhnev personally, do not want it. There is nothing in the divergent political interests of the two countries to necessitate or justify it.

If we insist on placing military considerations at the heart of our consideration and discussion of Soviet-American relations, we run a strong risk of eventually bringing about the very war we do not want and should be concerned to avoid. History shows that belief in the inevitability of war with a given power affects behavior in such a way as to cripple all constructive policy approaches towards that power, leaves the field open for military compulsions, and thus easily takes on the character of a self-fulfilling prophecy. A war regarded as inevitable or even probable, and therefore much prepared for, has a very good chance of eventually being fought.

Let us teach ourselves to look at the Soviet problem as a serious political one which has, indeed, military implications, but to bear in mind that these implications are of a secondary, not primary, nature; and let us not be hypnotized by military values to the point where we become blind to the others and fail to develop the hopeful and construc- tive possibilities of the relationship.

The greatest danger inherent in the existing competition between the Soviet Union and the United States in the military field is not the danger of a Soviet attack on ourselves or on NATO; it is the danger that the momentum of this tremendous and infinitely dangerous weapons race will get out of hand, will become wholly uncontrollable, and will, either through proliferation or by accident, carry us all to destruction. Even as things stand today, the sheer volume—the megatonnage—of nuclear explosives in our hands and in those of our Soviet adversaries is a menace to all mankind. It far exceeds what could conceivably be used to any good purpose, even in defense. It presents, I repeat, by the very fact of its existence, a danger greater than anything involved in the worst political possibilities of East-West relations. Our first task is to bring this situation under control. And this task begins with a restruc- turing of our own thinking.

9. The Failure to Understand Strategy

Edward N. Luttwak

In his Council on Foreign Relations speech (see selection 4), Kennan showed a disinclination to enter into questions of military calculus. In The Cloud of Danger *he goes one step further, implying that if peace can be maintained only by a balance of terror, it might be better to have no defense at all: "If an adequate NATO defense establishment can be created in Europe only at the cost of persuading people . . . that the best we can hope for in East-West relations is a military standoff of indefinite duration based on an atmosphere of total suspicion and hostility, then I am not sure that the effort to achieve such an establishment would not be self-defeating; for no real security is to be attained along that line."*

Edward N. Luttwak, who contests Kennan's reasoning about the strategic balance, is a research professor at Georgetown University and a senior fellow at the university's Center for Strategic and International Studies. He is the author of A Dictionary of Modern War *(1972),* The Grand Strategy of the Roman Empire *(1976), and the monograph* Strategic Power: Military Capability and Political Utility, *among other works on problems of military strategy.*

GEORGE F. KENNAN HAS SUFFICIENT CLAIM to be taken seriously when American foreign policy is discussed: indeed, many consider him the most eminent commentator on the subject. To his expressed discomfort, Mr. Kennan's widest public repute still derives from the 1947 "X" article in *Foreign Affairs*, which did duty as the great corrective to the willful delusion of Stalin's benevolence that the wartime alliance had engendered. By explaining that Soviet governance and Russian traditions would unfailingly conspire to force a brutal transition from alliance to outright hostility, regardless of any American concessions that might decently be offered, Mr. Kennan made himself the educator of the Truman administration, and the leading publicist of its Soviet policy.

Another man might have built enduring power on the sudden authority of his words, but Mr. Kennan's dominant emotion was already then a profound diffidence toward the enthusiasms of others; the same quality that had preserved his clear view of Russian realities while others were blinded by self-deception—and by the sincere solidarity of the struggle against Hitler—also prevented him from joining wholeheartedly in the great upsurge of energies of the Marshall Plan and the Atlantic Alliance. His time in the mainstream of policy was accordingly brief; in Dean Acheson, the State Department soon acquired a master who admired Mr. Kennan's intellect but who also distrusted his judgment. Mr. Kennan's further service as a diplomat was not undistinguished, but he had little role in the formulation of policy. Instead of making foreign policy, he was to write of its making, in more than a dozen books, several historical and of significant scholarship, and all elegantly written. These works perpetuate his influence.

It is therefore a matter of some consequence that Mr. Kennan is to a large degree an isolationist. Not, to be sure, a total isolationist, or one whose motives are those of the crude provincial who would have us ignore everything of which he is ignorant. Still less is Mr. Kennan one of the isolationists of the Left, whose interest in foreign affairs might be intense but who seek to diminish the role of America abroad because they see it as inherently evil. Mr. Kennan knows much about the world, and he does not regard his own country as malevolent. It is, however, his belief that the United States is ill-suited to the task of conducting a foreign policy of global dimensions; accordingly he advocates "the reduction of external commitments to the indispensable minimum." Mr. Kennan defines this "minimum" as "the preservation of the political independence and military security of Western Europe, of Japan, and—with the single reservation that it should not involve the dispatch and commitment of American armed forces—of Israel." This strategic prescription comes at the end of Mr. Kennan's latest book, *The Cloud of Danger*, a work prompted by his feeling that we have reached "a crucial parting of the ways: one road leading to a total militarization of policy, . . . the other to an effort to break out of the straight jacket of military rivalry and to strike through to a more constructive and hopeful vision of America's future and the world's." The diverse essays of Mr. Kennan's new book cover all but a few of the concerns of an American Secretary of State. There are separate sections on no fewer than eighteen countries whose affairs are now of special interest for one reason or another (neither Canada nor Israel rates a section), and three whole chapters are devoted to the Soviet Union and U.S.-Soviet relations. One, subtitled "The Alarm," largely deals with the military power of the Soviet Union as seen, or perhaps as merely portrayed, by the "vociferous band" who have "an interest of one sort or another in military expenditures; those whose long-standing dream had been to see the United States committed to the overthrow of Soviet power; and those for whom a ringing show of anti-Communist belligerence and vigilance was the stock of political trade." Mr. Kennan does allow that there are others, "wholly unselfish and dedicated in motive," who also persist in fearing the growth of Soviet military power, but they are said to be blinded by a "highly bipolar view of international problems." The second chapter on the Soviet Union, subtitled "The Reality," naturally presents Mr. Kennan's own view of Russia.

Mr. Kennan recognizes the "functional" issues also, in a chapter in which he writes of the "Impending Food Population Crisis," of environmental problems, and so on. It is in this chapter that Mr. Kennan is at his best and at his worst, in dealing with OPEC and the Third World, and with "Democracy as a World Cause" respectively. He neatly deflates the emotive dysfunction that passes for enlightened opinion on the subject of the Third World and its peremptory monetary claims for imaginary wrongs. But then there comes his already notorious view that democracy is the exclusive possession of northwestern Europeans, in place or transplanted. There is no need to condemn this view; hundreds of millions of Indians have already given it the fullest possible refutation. In countless translated interviews in print and on television, simple Indian villagers have offered evidence of the essential universality of the democratic ideal, and have explained that ideal with a clarity that many an American college student might profitably emulate.

A Manufactured Threat?

There is one theme that emerges again and again throughout Mr. Kennan's book: the essentially chimerical nature of the military threats that are said to face us, which Mr. Kennan invariably sees as manufactured by the self-interested or at least as very greatly exaggerated, and the persistent insinuation that military power can never truly serve to protect our interests and ideals. One sees why Mr. Kennan retains a wide following among those still called liberals who are more precisely described as "defense minimalists," or more simply as "doves." But the constituency that would accept Mr. Kennan's self-denying strategic formula is actually far broader. Even many who find value in the military instrument in our foreign policy are attracted by the neat economy of Mr. Kennan's Western Europe–Japan perimeter, with Israel somewhat insecurely attached. In fact, in the strategic literature of the post-Vietnam years there has been much cutting and pasting of the world map in search of "optimal perimeters," complete with consumer-reports assessments of the desirability of including this or that country (Mr. Kennan, for example, defines his Western Europe very restrictively, and would view with favor the departure of Greece and Turkey from NATO).

It should come as no surprise that the glorified bookkeepers ("systems analysts") and managerial types in uniform who nowadays pass for strategists should indulge themselves playing with maps and drawing perimeter lines. But Mr. Kennan is also a competent historian, and he should know better: the exercise is inherently futile. The legitimate sphere of strategy is to define risks and costs, and the choices between them: is country X to be protected by an active defense which requires forces in place and corresponding expenditure, or is X to be protected by deterrence, which requires no additional forces but which entails a built-in escalation risk? Or, on a smaller scale, is the entire territory of X to be guarded by large and costly forces that can actually keep out an invader, or should the forces deployed forward suffice only to hold some part of X with an invader being driven out only *after* the fact, by forces brought from elsewhere?

At many levels and in many ways these are the questions that fall within our calculated choice. But there is no such freedom in determining whether X should be protected at all. The strategic goals of foreign policy are not to be decided by exercises in definition; they are defined for us by the very nature of our country, and by the circumstances of world politics. There are always those who will try to define *ab initio* an optimal set of strategic goals, as Mr. Kennan does, but such definitions are of no consequence.

It will be recalled that by 1950, both the civil and the military officials of the U.S. government had agreed that South Korea should be excluded from the American security perimeter in the Pacific. The decision was formally made and duly registered in the official planning documents. To the managerial mind, the exclusion of Korea was eminently sensible. As a non-industrial state with an overcrowded countryside, Korea's intrinsic worth was then small; on the other hand, since Korea is part of the East Asian mainland, it could not be fully defended with air and naval forces alone, America's strong suit; finally, South Korea seemed to have a relentless enemy in the North Korean regime. The low benefit, high possible costs, and high risks made the calculation very simple, while the absence of a powerful Korean-American community meant that the managerial decision would not be overturned by unreasoned congressional pressures.

Then, in the early morning of June 25, 1950, North Korean troops attacked across the North-South demarcation line. South Korea was still very poor; the peninsula was still irremediably attached to the Asian mainland, and its rescue would now undoubtedly require American troops on the ground; and the number of Korean-Americans ready to write to their Congressman had not appreciably increased. Nothing of relevance to the original decision had changed at all, and yet the policy was utterly overturned, precisely when the North Korean invasion made it operative. For it was then suddenly realized that the United States had become a Pacific power, and since the Pacific is unfortunately empty of significant land masses, the American perimeter would of necessity have to be withdrawn to the shores of Western America unless it rested on the East Asian rim (Hawaii and the islands of Micronesia could be no more than outposts). Finally, it could justifiably be feared that Japan would not allow itself to be held if the United States were to accept the conquest of South Korea without effective challenge: as soon as the end of the occupation allowed it to do so, Japan would extrude an American protector which did not protect. Hence the total and immediate reversal of the decision, and the large war that followed, which a firm American commitment clearly stated might well have averted.

A Lesson Forgotten

As a senior participant, Mr. Kennan should have retained a clear memory of the Korean war, and should have pondered its deeper lessons. And yet he would now have us repeat the error. In *The Cloud of Danger,* he writes that the circumstances of 1950 do not obtain. "There is a fully independent and stable Japanese government. . . . Power in Moscow is in the hands of people who, whatever one thinks of them, represent a great change from the Soviet regime of Stalin's last years. It is doubtful that either Moscow or Peking wants to see at this juncture the sort of crisis that would be introduced by a renewal of civil war in Korea. To this must be added a very unhappy and disturbing factor: namely, the nature and behavior of the Park regime. . . ." He ends by prescribing a withdrawal. All that he writes is quite true, but quite marginal to the issue. A second Korean war would not be started by the rulers of Moscow or Peking but rather by Kim Il Sung, and whatever one may think of him, he does not represent a great change from the Kim Il Sung of 1950. As for Japan, it is undoubtedly stable but also, as Mr. Kennan writes, "fully independent" and as such likely to be entirely unwilling to be left isolated, and thus fully exposed to a still inimical China, a rabid Korea, and an always dangerous Soviet Union, protected only by constantly diminishing American naval and air forces.

Elsewhere in his book Mr. Kennan is eloquent on the importance of Japan, and quite rightly points out the grave dangers that would face us if the export capacity of the Japanese were to be redirected from civilian production for the West to military production for China or the Soviet Union, or both. Unfortunately one cannot order à la carte; the Japanese undoubtedly much prefer alliance with the United States, but they can hardly continue indefinitely to consign their security to our hands if we persevere in dismantling the military strength which is their protection. If forced to do so, they will reach a more secure accommodation with others. The Japanese share Mr. Kennan's distaste for the practices of the Park regime, but no amount of student-bashing in South Korea will lead them to prefer a Communist united Korea across the narrow straits from their home islands. If Mr. Kennan wants to order Japan, he must follow the set menu and have South Korea also. As a historian of Russian foreign policy, Mr. Kennan should have recalled the example of another and greater illusion of free choice. The foreign policy of the Bolsheviks newly returned from exile was announced to the world in 1918 as entirely revolutionary: the Russian people would allow freedom to all the peripheral nationalities and the new Russian state would abjure expansion, renounce war and secret diplomacy, and rely instead on the class solidarity of the workers of the world. Yet in spite of the drastic change in the governance and entire society of Russia achieved by the revolution, the one thing that did not in the end change at all was precisely Russian foreign policy. All those millions of words spoken in the hopeful discussions of exile, all the pamphlets, speeches, and declarations, even the actual policies briefly followed immediately after Lenin's seizure of power, could not transcend the nature of the country and the circumstances of world politics. Very soon Soviet foreign policy became a perfectly direct continuation of the expansion program of Peter the Great and all the Czars. In the Soviet case also, the real strategic choices have been between costs and risks in the pursuit of goals given rather than chosen.

And of course in Mao's China also there has been a parallel reversion, in spite of radical change in all else. Today Peking tries to build a sphere of client states and seeks to divide powerful barbarians in a manner entirely traditional: in fact, even the classic procedures of the Middle Kingdom's diplomacy remain, with foreign envoys being received in Peking quite frequently while Chinese envoys rarely deign to return the visits. Nuclear deterrence must now replace the Great Wall, and the Chinese now worry about the inadequacy of their tanks instead of the traditional inferiority of their cavalry, but for all that, the Chinese policy-maker who would consult the ancient manuals of statecraft would not be indulging in mere antiquarian affectation. No amount of ideological invocation can alter the basic predicament of China, which must still determine its conduct in international affairs.

Mr. Kennan is undoubtedly aware of all this, and yet he has obviously failed to construe its meaning for our foreign policy: for the United States also, circumstances impose strategic goals which cannot arbitrarily be diminished to Mr. Kennan's "indispensable minimum." The attempt to limit effort by defining a narrow perimeter of responsibility may well invite aggression against all that is left out, and it will assuredly fail to limit the costs and risks of protecting what is left in. Neither what might be called the banker's perimeter (which happens to be Mr. Kennan's also), marked out by the clustering of high incomes per capita, nor the racial perimeter that would include Australia and New Zealand while perhaps excluding Japan, nor the raw-materials perimeter that would include the Persian Gulf but not Israel, has any meaning in the reality of world politics.

Power, Not Perimeters

For it is the balance of power alone that will unfailingly determine what can be protected and how securely, and not any predetermined perimeter of convenience defined in the abstract. It is the relative military strength, economic leverage, and social influence of the United States as compared to its antagonists that defines the scope of American protection, influence, and access. If the United States continues to allow its relative military power to decline as compared to that of its antagonists, and principally the Soviet Union, sooner or later it may well be forced to retreat into Mr. Kennan's restricted perimeter, if not beyond.

But the reverse does not obtain; if the United States were to abandon all but Western Europe and Japan, this would not allow it to reduce its military power with impunity, as Mr. Kennan seems to believe. On the contrary, the industrial democracies under siege would probably need much more military power than they now have, merely to survive.

The crude tactical analogy that underlies all the post-Vietnam perimeter strategies, as well as those classically isolationist, does not resist scrutiny. The suggestion is that a smaller area of responsibility can be protected with smaller military forces, just as a smaller body of soldiers may suffice to hold a shorter defense line. But this is only true if the enemy gains no power from the terrain abandoned. Had Hitler been given a free hand to organize Europe, he would most probably have emerged from an eventual continental victory with both nuclear weapons and long-range missiles, thus nullifying the naval defense on which the isolationist strategy depended. If the Soviet Union were now given a free run all over the world but for Western Europe and Japan, it too would eventually nullify Western defenses, by exploiting raw-material vulnerabilities and also by controlling the sea lanes between Western Europe and Japan, if not between the United States and both. Before any defenses were so reduced, it is more than likely that the United States would find itself quite alone, since both the nations of Western Europe and Japan would in prudence reach accommodation with Russia.

The appropriate tactical analogy is quite different from the one underlying the post-Vietnam perimeter strategies. If unopposed, even a small body of soldiers can dominate much territory, but if faced by superior strength it may not be able to defend even a cluster of foxholes. And so it is for us: the determining factor in setting the minimum level of our own military effort is the rising military power of our antagonists, and chiefly the Soviet Union, and the cost to us cannot unfortunately be contained by any arbitrary geographic limitation of our responsibilities. This is not a pretty state of affairs, but Mr. Kennan's formula will not assist us in evading the predicament that unavoidably became ours when Britain's decline and the collapse of France left the United States as the chief protector of its own interests.

Mr. Kennan's opinions on the Third World and the North-South issues are eminently sensible; his analysis of the oil-price crisis and OPEC is replete with hard truths that deserve close attention; on many other questions large and small, from Southern Africa to the Panama Canal and from international economic policy to the procedures of our diplomacy, Mr. Kennan's book reveals the wisdom of long experience and high intellect combined. Why then the gross misconception of his overall strategy which undermines his good advice on particular matters?

As in the case of so many of our opinion-makers, Mr. Kennan is motivated by an overwhelming desire to diminish the absolute magnitude of American military power. It is perhaps symptomatic that his first words on the subject on the ninth page of the book are headed by the tired cliché, "Military-Industrial Complex," and that the quality of Mr. Kennan's prose suffers markedly whenever he writes of military things. He begins by noting that 6 per cent of the total national product is now absorbed by "the Pentagon." Since the major potential antagonists of the United States are now devoting much higher percentages of their GNP's to defense, the 6 per cent should be the subject of much self-congratulation. But Mr. Kennan's standards are his own, and do not reflect the circumstances of the world; his attitude is severe. He proceeds to argue that military expenditures are strongly inflationary because of "the lavish way in which money is used, as compared with functions that are obliged to meet the normal competition of private life."

Mr. Kennan informs the reader that he has lately found confirmation for his views. "Having written this, I note the following passage from an article . . . by Mr. Seymour Melman, Professor of Industrial Engineering at Columbia University." And he quotes. Characteristically, Mr. Kennan, who is otherwise so careful in choosing the few authorities he cites, slips badly when he quotes on military things. Mr. Kennan is obviously unaware that his authority is not a disinterested scholar driven to write by some late discovery, but rather a full-time critic of the military establishment, willing to attack any defense project on economic, environmental, diplomatic, or moral grounds interchangeably, and who would no doubt oppose defense expenditures just as strongly even if by some miracle their effect were to be deflationary.

Mr. Kennan next issues an admonition: those who are concerned with the military balance should "give more attention to . . . inflation . . . and less to efforts to convince the rest of us of the menacing intentions and fearful strength of our Soviet opponents." More of the same follows in a rather personal vein and in sub-standard prose ("One time, when I was . . . watching several forms of target practice, I was struck by the realization that each one of a certain class of missiles that were being fired off with great abandon . . . cost more than my entire Pennsylvania farm").

One would have imagined that Mr. Kennan the historian would remember that historically the United States has grossly underspent on defense. With forces too small to deter war in 1939 and 1941, the United States was compelled thereafter to field troops with inferior weapons in many cases, because of drastic pre-war economies that restricted the development of new weapons. It was not, for example, until 1943 that the United States acquired fighter aircraft that could match those of the Germans and Japanese, and it was not until the last weeks of World War II that American troops received tanks that could fight those of the Germans on even terms. And in Korea again American troops found themselves ill-equipped in fighting much poorer enemies because of the extreme economies of the pre-conflict defense budgets. One recognizes the enormity of firing million-dollar missiles for target practice, but it would be no less outrageous if the soldiers of the richest society on earth were once again to face their enemies recklessly unprovided.

Misunderstanding Military Power

For all the emotional intensity that Mr. Kennan's words reveal when he is writing on the subject, it would be unfair to suggest that his refusal to give military power its due reflects only an emotional revulsion. Of equal significance is Mr. Kennan's honest inability to appreciate the role of military power in the broader context of foreign policy, as well as a peculiar difficulty in understanding even the simplest technical aspects of modern military power, on which he nevertheless writes at some length.

The clearest example of his first and decisive shortcoming occurs in his comments on European security:

> With respect to the Soviet Union there has been established in the minds of many of the Europeans a certain fixed pattern of thought . . . [which] consists in the unshakable belief: (1) that Soviet leaders are keenly desirous of launching an attack on Western Europe; (2) that without the commitment of America's nuclear power neither the Western Europeans, nor they and the Americans together, would have the faintest chance of resisting successfully an onslaught of this nature . . .; and (3) that the Russians have been deterred from launching such an attack only by the threat of American nuclear retaliation.

Now what is really very remarkable about these propositions is that they bear no relationship to any seriously representative European views. First, the Europeans plainly have *not* regarded a Soviet attack as imminent, otherwise they would no doubt have been willing to devote greater resources for their own defense. In fact, it was only in 1950-52 that there was among many Europeans genuine fear of a Soviet attack, a fear prompted by the all too real attack in Korea. Ever since then it has always been the *Americans* who have stressed the immediacy of the Soviet threat in NATO councils, while the European view has always been distinctly more relaxed. It is quite astonishing that Mr. Kennan should ignore the amply documented record on this matter, with which even the most casual observers of NATO are familiar.

His second proposition is also entirely in error: the Europeans have never believed that a Soviet attack could only be resisted by American nuclear weapons. Rather, they quite rightly prefer a strategy that would seek to avert war by nuclear *deterrence*—which puts the lives of Russians and Americans at risk together with their own—as opposed to a strategy of non-nuclear *defense*, in which the rival armies would prepare to fight it out in the fields and cities of Central Europe with great destruction, while Russian and American civil life would remain unattacked.

In the third proposition, Mr. Kennan has his Europeans believing that a Russian invasion has been prevented so far only by American nuclear deterrence. But European views on this point are diverse; once again, it has always been the Americans who have taken the more pessimistic view. The military threat of the Soviet armies now poised to attack Europe is not to be dismissed, but as Mr. Kennan himself acknowledges, this has not been the operative consideration. It is not the eventual, one-time threat of an attack that must concern us, Europeans and Americans alike, but rather the permanent impact of Soviet military power on the Europeans' freedom of political action. NATO may or may not have deterred a war otherwise contemplated, but it has certainly served to deny the Russians the dominant political influence over Western Europe which they undoubtedly keenly desire. It is odd to find that the unmilitary Mr. Kennan thinks only of the potential combat role of military forces and does not appreciate their continuing political function. The Russians now successfully employ their military forces to overawe Eastern Europe into a reluctant obedience, and they actively seek a measure of political control over Western Europe as well. Indeed it is only natural that they should try: lacking economic leverage, cultural influence, or social appeal, they must do what they can with their one effective source of power. At one point Mr. Kennan satirizes this prosaic view of Soviet intentions, but nowhere does he refute it in reasoned discourse.

It would be unkind to list every example of Mr. Kennan's inability to comprehend the technical military questions on which he writes. Indeed, one is tempted in courtesy to avoid the subject altogether. But of late it has become quite customary for the wholly unqualified to pass judgment on matters which require an irreducible minimum of technical competence, and if these pretensions are left unchallenged, questions already highly complex will needlessly be further confused by avoidable errors of fact. One instance suffices. In discussing nuclear testing, Mr. Kennan argues that the United States should offer to ban all tests, on a basis of reciprocity with the Soviet Union. Others may differ, but as in the case of any complex strategic issue, there is room for entirely legitimate disagreement. But then Mr. Kennan goes on to write: ". . . the main purpose of these tests, as now pursued, is to find some gimmick that will suddenly give us an edge over the Russians. . . . And this is exactly the kind of thinking that is going to have to stop, if this mad proliferation of nuclear destructive power is ever to be halted and reversed."

Mr. Kennan's emotional appeal is inspired by a gross error of fact. The "main purpose" of American nuclear testing is not now, and has not been for many years, to find "some gimmick" that would give us an advantage over the Russians. The main purpose of American nuclear testing is in fact to validate for production safer and *less* destructive weapons in order to minimize fallout as well as unnecessary damage off-target, and more particularly to reduce the risk of accidental or unauthorized explosions.

Thus, for example, the standard strategic bomb of today is very much less powerful than the bombs of the early 1960's, while having on the other hand altogether more reliable safety and control devices. It is not the hope of gaining an advantage over the Russians that motivates the work of the laboratories at Los Alamos and elsewhere, but rather the knowledge that much remains to be done to reduce further the risk of unintended explosions. When a man of some eminence commits to print purported statements of fact, his readers are entitled to assume that he has made reasonable efforts to insure accuracy. Information on the purposes of American nuclear-weapons development is widely available, and Mr. Kennan could have avoided the error for the price of a few minutes of cursory reading.

View From the Log House

But there is also another quite different and altogether more legitimate basis of Mr. Kennan's strategy of qualified isolationism. In persuasively challenging the notion that the industrialized world is somehow responsible for the poverty of the Third World, and that it must now correct the disparity by sacrificing its own prosperity, Mr. Kennan evokes a memory of his native Wisconsin:

> I have before me, as I write, a faded snapshot, . . . of the log house in which my great-grandparents lived when they first came in 1851, to the Green Bay region of Wisconsin: a crude, almost windowless structure, standing in a dreary treeless field. And I am moved to recall that the Wisconsin of that day was very much what we today would call an underdeveloped country. Well, these people worked hard, and . . . Wisconsin prospered . . . under

their ministrations. . . . Had we Wisconsinites been a lazy, violent, improvident people, devoted more to war than to industry—had we wasted what little substance we had on civil strife of one sort or another, or had we been for other reasons unsuccessful . . . would we today be seen as the possessors of a peculiar virtue vis-à-vis the more developed countries entitling us to put claims on their beneficence and to demand of them that they exert themselves to promote our development? . . . And is no credit whatsoever to be given in this modern world for the old-fashioned American virtues of thrift, honesty, tolerance, civic discipline, and hard work?

Here, then, are the classic roots of the isolationist position, revealed in the course of a quite unanswerable argument against the white guilt complex and its absurdities. Like the Orthodox Jew who on Passover thanks the Lord for saving him—and not just his ancestors—from the Egyptian bondage, and who gives thanks for his own safe conveyance across the Red Sea, Mr. Kennan too identifies with the pioneer experience. He sees himself driven by persecution or poverty from the Old World to the wilderness of America, only to find that as soon as he has by hard work, self-sacrifice, and civic virtue created wealth and tranquility, the Old World begins to make demands upon the strength and prosperity of the New—demands which reflect precisely the Old World's failure to avoid war and "civil strife."

These are not sentiments that can lightly be dismissed. There is so much natural beauty and man-made wealth in America, still so much opportunity for creative pursuits, and still so much scope for individual action, that concern for the outside world may easily seem a costly and entirely dispensable burden. Even those who lack snapshots of great-grandparental log houses are apt to suffer from the temptation to cast this burden off. Unfortunately, it is the modern predicament of America that the only practical strategy is one of involvement. The security of America itself must derive from a tolerable balance of power with its potential adversaries, and a balance of power is more easily maintained with allies than without. An America without allies could undoubtedly avoid the dangers of peripheral conflicts fought in their defense, but it would ultimately be exposed to the formidable threat of some regime, probably Soviet, which had organized the resources of all Europe and beyond to muster inordinate strength against the United States. And an America without allies would even before then have to suffer the demoralization of seeing its own values repudiated and scorned in other lands, as well as a sense of psychic isolation so intense that it would be shared by all but the most insular of Americans, and certainly by intellectuals such as Mr. Kennan.

If the necessity of an immediate circle of allies is recognized, as it is in Mr. Kennan's minimalist formula, the logic of collective security, the regional concerns of each primary ally, and the maintenance of a global balance of power will certainly require a further and wider sphere of secondary involvement. This is not a desirable chain of necessities for America, since the pursuits of power are inherently sterile. But it is the clear lesson of the century that any attempt to evade our strategic predicament unfailingly entails a heavy price in blood and treasure. That is why we must reject Mr. Kennan's counsel of evasion.

10. Kennan's Grand Design

Eugene V. Rostow

✧ ✧ ✧ ✧ ✧ ✧ ✧ ✧ ✧ ✧ ✧ ✧ ✧ ✧ ✧ ✧

Mr. Rostow is Sterling Professor of Law and Public Affairs at Yale University, but he wants the reader to know that his critique of George Kennan bears a direct relationship to his position as Chairman of the Executive Committee of the Committee on the Present Danger, which was formed in 1976 and whose policies are attacked in Kennan's The Cloud of Danger. *Mr. Rostow was Under Secretary of State for Political Affairs from 1966 through 1969.*

Professor Rostow insists that Kennan is no ordinary scholar or diplomat: "Kennan is an impressionist, a poet, not an earthling," yet he is "one of our most important and influential" foreign policy writers. Appraising The Cloud of Danger, *Mr. Rostow says: "Kennan's sad new book perfectly portrays a fashionable post-Vietnam mood about foreign affairs. Exhausted, disillusioned, and nearly without hope . . . he comes perilously close to preaching that we don't really need a foreign and defense policy at all. In essence, Kennan argues that we should disarm unilaterally, save for our conventional forces in Europe."*

✧ ✧ ✧ ✧ ✧ ✧ ✧ ✧ ✧ ✧ ✧ ✧ ✧ ✧ ✧ ✧

Reprinted by permission of The Yale Journal Company, Fred B. Rothman & Company, and the author from *The Yale Law Journal*, Volume 87, pages 1527-1548 (June 1978); the article appeared there under the title "Searching for Kennan's Grand Design." Footnotes deleted by permission of the author.

GEORGE KENNAN'S CAREER is divided into two more or less distinct periods. During the first, he was a conspicuous and rather controversial foreign service officer and then ambassador, and one of the State Department's leading intellectuals, especially as an expert on Russia and the Soviet Union. Since 1953, with short interludes back in harness, he has been a member of the Institute for Advanced Study at Princeton, a Visiting Professor at Oxford and Chicago, and a prolific writer and lecturer about foreign affairs.

Kennan is a grave person, what the French call *sérieux*, a man of character and sensibility absorbed in the quest for the ultimate. His books and articles have attracted a wide following, and have been crowned with many prizes. With felicitous sympathy, Kennan's writings express the yearnings and anxieties of his readers about the role of the United States in world politics. Now, in *The Cloud of Danger*, he has written a testament of faith—a compendium of advice about what he thinks our foreign policy should be, and how we should seek to fulfill it.

It is easy to dismiss the bulk of Kennan's work on foreign policy as confused, inconsistent, and detached from the most objective measures of reality, and many have done so. In this respect, *The Cloud of Danger* is not an exception. The book is elusive. And its counsel of American neutrality and isolation is addressed to the world as it was before 1914, when the Concert of Europe maintained a generally stable system of world politics, and the British fleet stood between the United States and the risks of catastrophic change in the world balance of power.

Within their limits, academic criticisms of Kennan's work along these lines are justified. But they miss its most significant quality. Kennan is an impressionist, a poet, not an earthling. His mind has never moved along mathematical lines, and never will. A careful reader can parse only one of his major papers—his celebrated article, "The Sources of Soviet Conduct," published in 1947 in *Foreign Affairs* under the signature *X*. During the intervening thirty years, Kennan has frequently explained that he did not mean what the article by *X* so plainly said.

Despite the casualness and ambiguity of Kennan's methods—or perhaps because of them—he is one of our most important and influential writers about foreign policy. His books, articles, and lectures are persuasive and convincing, not in mapping new theories about reality or in outlining new strategies for policy, but in articulating states of feeling that were parts of the national consciousness at the time he wrote.

Thus some of his best work has expressed the widespread sympathy of the American people for the aims of the Russian Revolution. And in 1947, Kennan gave voice to the sense that we should somehow "contain" Soviet expansion, after Western public opinion had come to realize that our ardent hopes for post-war political cooperation with the Soviet Union were unrequited. Kennan's article signed X was part of the background for the most creative period in the modern history of our foreign policy—the period of the Marshall Plan and other measures for speeding the economic recovery of the industrialized democracies and the formation of Europe and later of OECD; the Point Four policy of assistance to the developing nations; the Baruch Plan for the international control of atomic energy; and the Truman Doctrine, NATO, the Korean War and other steps for consolidating a system of peace based on a stable balance of power, and the proposition that peace on our small, interdependent, and dangerous planet is "indivisible."

Kennan's sad new book perfectly portrays a fashionable post-Vietnam mood about foreign affairs. Exhausted, disillusioned, and nearly without hope, Kennan says "Good-bye to All That." He comes perilously close to preaching that we don't really need a foreign and defense policy at all. In essence, Kennan argues that we should disarm unilaterally, save for our conventional forces in Europe. He seems to believe that our strategic commitments and deployments exceed the sphere of our interests, and favors an American withdrawal from many regions of the world. In dealing with the Soviet Union, Kennan would have us apply diplomatic persuasion and the power of a good example rather than deterrent military strength. The goal of our efforts, he urges, should be to coax that country away from paranoid fears of encirclement, and from any lingering traces of imperial and ideological ambition it may be conceded to harbor. Given the nature of the Russian and Soviet culture, Kennan insists, Soviet policy—at least since Stalin's death—cannot be aggressive. It is planned and carried out by elderly, conservative bureaucrats, who are primarily concerned, he says, with the preservation of their power in the Soviet Union and Eastern Europe. He finds them defensive, cautious, prudent, suspicious, and difficult, but not aggressive elsewhere. In urging this view of Soviet conduct, Kennan ignores or dismisses the evidence about Soviet behavior since 1972 inconsistent with his thesis: Soviet support for the breach of the 1973 agreements for peace in Indochina; for India's attack on Pakistan in 1972; for the Arab aggression against Israel in 1973; and for the long cycle of aggressive warfare now being waged in many parts of Africa. I say that Kennan comes perilously close to advising his countrymen to pursue a foreign policy of benign passivity, because that is the thrust of eighty percent of his text. But the book includes a number of what Dean Rusk calls "Pearl Harbor passages"—precautionary caveats to protect the writer against the charge of having misread the portents if events should take an unpleasant turn. In these passages, Kennan admits that Soviet policy may turn hostile and expansionist after all— especially if we offer irresistible temptation through weakness and confusion, or goad the Russians into aggression by "destabilizing" actions like improving our weapons systems. And he clearly believes that beyond repelling invaders the United States does have national security interests in world politics worth protecting by the use of military force if necessary. According to Kennan's analysis, these interests are not numerous, but there are a few: the protection of the industrial parts of North-Western Europe, for example, and perhaps of Japan; and, most surprisingly, the maintenance of an overall strategic and conventional force balance vis-à-vis the Soviet Union. Kennan thinks we should sympathize with Israel, but never use force to save it from destruction.

As for the rest of the agenda of foreign affairs, Kennan's policy is old-fashioned nineteenth-century isolationism, diluted occasionally by flashes of nineteenth-century irritation, and a nineteenth-century impulse to command the respect of lesser breeds by sending the gun boats. We should leave the struggling nations of the Third World to their melancholy and incurable fate, he urges, and let the Chinese and the Soviets fight it out, if they are so inclined, without running any risks to prevent a Sino-Soviet War, or to influence its outcome.

Contradictions of this kind have always been characteristic of Kennan's work. As readers of his *Memoirs* will recall, he has suffered throughout his life from conflicts he has been unable to resolve—conflicts about himself, his dream world, his work, his goals, and his relationship to the American nation and culture. Like Brooks Adams and James Fenimore Cooper, George Kennan is a member of the worthy tribe of nay-sayers who are as necessary to a healthy society as yeast is to bread, or sand to pearls. Like Adams and Cooper, Kennan is preoccupied with the American culture, but deeply ambivalent about it—drawn and repelled at the same time, and quite unable to ignore it, or indeed to accept it as it is.

Brought up in a modest middle-class home in Milwaukee, the young Kennan went to Princeton in 1921—the cheerful, Philistine, country club Princeton of Scott Fitzgerald's time. There he felt alien and isolated—clubless, an outsider. Entering the foreign service in 1926, Kennan was soon drawn into an imaginative program for training specialists in Soviet affairs, and spent a number of years in Riga and other posts far from the mainstream of the service during that period, basically a research student rather than an active participant in the life of the Department. When we established diplomatic relations with the Soviet Union in 1933, Kennan and his fellow Russian experts in the service—Thompson, Bohlen, and Kohler—became marked men and moved to the center of the stage.

Early in his career, Puritan lineaments alien to the Princeton model emerged as dominant in Kennan's personality. He saw himself as part of the intellectual and moral Puritan aristocracy of Hawthorne's imagination. Kennan has a high specific gravity, and the assurance of a man anointed. He speaks ex cathedra, often severely, and sometimes he excommunicates.

From his Puritan vantage point, Kennan has excoriated what he regards as the vulgarity, materialism, and bad taste of the American culture; its deplorably simplistic and irrational politics; its affinity for demagogues and mountebanks; and its increasing alienation from the true sources of moral purity—the life of small agricultural communities, where men were self-reliant and worked hard, in constant contact with the earth and with animals, and women did the laundry together at the village pump, or on the banks of a stream. In developing these favorite themes, Kennan can never fall back on the satire, ridicule, humor, and gusto of other famous American nay-sayers like Mark Twain, H. L. Mencken, or Sinclair Lewis. These gifts are not in this armory.

Handicaps to U.S. Foreign Policy

The Cloud of Dangers is framed by a gloomy and characteristic first chapter, explaining why the United States is incapable of a rational and effective foreign policy and perhaps beyond redemption in any event. The themes of the first chapter permeate the book.

First, Kennan argues, our Constitution makes it impossible for the United States to carry out a wide-ranging, great-power foreign policy. The Constitution works well enough to permit a united nation to protect its own shores against invasion; it is too cumbersome and diffuse, however, to allow us to carry out more complex policies.

To Kennan's way of thinking, the conduct of foreign affairs is a technical matter that should be left to the experts—that is, to the professionals. They know best. The President can be allowed some supervisory jurisdiction, but not much. And Congress should be kept in its place altogether. Our Constitution and its doctrine of the separation of powers, Kennan writes, deny our government "the privacy, the flexibility, and the promptness and incisiveness of decision and action, which have marked the great imperial powers of the past and which are generally considered necessary to the conduct of an effective world policy by the rulers of a great state."

Our posture in this regard, he thinks, has become worse in recent years. The increasing size of the nation and the diversity of its government make the conduct of foreign policy by a small band of foreign service officers inconceivable. And Vietnam and Watergate have encouraged Congress to bid for power at the expense of the Presidency. Kennan argues that this state of affairs has the disadvantage of reducing the influence of the professionals, whom he portrays in idealized terms as the embodiment of insight, experience, scholarship, and flair. At the same time, Kennan argues, the post-Nixon trends of congressional assertion enhance the influence of the politicians, many of whom play hob with our foreign policy by their crude enthusiasm for "ethnic" causes.

Second, Kennan contends, the weight of what he calls the military-industrial complex in our affairs is disastrous to the possibility of having a wise and farsighted foreign policy. The military are wasteful in their habits, even when they are honest. In a phrase that reveals much about Kennan's blindness to the military element in history, he comments that the soldiers' habit of playing with "expensive toys" in peacetime is an addiction, so that it is nearly impossible to distinguish "the real needs of national defense" from the addictive ones. Kennan has never accepted the Roman maxim "si vis pacem, pare bellum."

Third, our increasing dependence on the developing countries for oil and other raw materials is a growing handicap to the nation as an ambitious actor on the world scene. Kennan regards it as "shameful" that we are unwilling to take firm measures against OPEC and comparable cartels to assure respect for ourselves and our interests. Since such policies seem beyond our psychological reach, he argues strongly for programs to assure our independence in energy and raw materials, whatever their cost.

Fourth, Kennan contends that the nation is weakened in its foreign relations by what he regards as its social and moral disintegration at home. Like most other middle-class members of the intellectual elite, Kennan feels bitterly threatened by recent developments with regard to crime, sex, pornography, drugs, and manners. He protests vehemently against inflation, strikes, the weakening of educational standards, the decline of the work ethic, the rise of the welfare state, television dominated by advertisers, inadequate systems of public transportation, environmental deterioration, and other familiar grievances. To restore the moral fiber of the nation, Kennan believes, will require an enormous, expensive, far-reaching effort, which should include steps to reverse some aspects of the industrial revolution, shifts from factory to handicraft production, and the removal of people from cities to the countryside.

This is an odd way to start a book about foreign policy, but its importance to George Kennan's mode of thought cannot be exaggerated. An academic book about foreign policy normally would begin with a geopolitical analysis of our national interest in the changing realm of world politics. *The Cloud of Danger* contains no such analysis, and its premises in this regard have to be isolated by nearly archeological procedures, which I shall attempt to apply later in this review. Instead, Kennan's overture is a proclamation that we are nearly doomed by our selfishness, materialism, and vulgarity, and so encumbered by our excessively democratic Constitution that it will probably be impossible for our civilized natural aristocracy to save the nation in any event. To recall Brooks Adams again, Kennan perceives an accelerating process of degradation at work in democracy. In Great Britain, democratic excess has already brought about an alarming condition, in his view, and the United States is not far behind. Confronting what he feels to be a rush toward the abyss, problems of foreign policy appear to be secondary, and nearly unmanageable.

Kennan outdoes the Prophets. However sharply they scolded the ancient Israelites for their sins and other shortcomings, not even Jeremiah despaired of their survival.

Two themes in Kennan's preliminary chorus of grievances require special attention in the perspective of foreign policy: his claims (1) that the influence of "the military-industrial complex" prevents us from taking advantage of diplomatic opportunities "to break out of the strait-jacket of military rivalry and to strike through to a more constructive and hopeful vision of America's future and the world's," and (2) that the constitutional role of Congress makes it impossible for the United States to function effectively as a great power.

I disagree strongly with Kennan on both these points, which are fundamental to his argument. Kennan's first thesis is an invocation of fashionable bogeymen. The supposed influence of the military-indus-trial complex has not prevented a considerable and unilateral disarma-ment of the United States since 1969. Kennan contends, however, that if we exclude the military element from the Soviet-American relation-ship diplomacy alone would induce the Soviet Union to accept a bal-anced, businesslike, and peaceful way of life with the United States. The best answer to Kennan's claim is to be found in some of his earlier writings, where he denies that the serious and principled men who direct the Communist movement and the Soviet Union can be induced to reach agreement through new formulae, one-sided gestures of con-fidence and generosity, or new approaches divorced from the problem of military deterrence. Given the nature of Russian culture and the Soviet system, Kennan has argued elsewhere, there is no possibility of a stable and constructive political understanding between the United States and the Soviet Union except one that is based on an assured balance of military power.

Kennan's second, constitutional argument should not be left unan-swered. This argument derives, I should contend, from a superficial view of the American Constitution and of the standards it establishes for the political process. The American Constitution is a robust and strenuous affair, and so is the democratic political process it attempts to govern. Of course we are going through a period of congressional assertiveness at the moment, in the aftermath of Nixon. But that fact does not make the United States ungovernable. The constitutional sys-tem that permitted the nation to survive slavery and the Civil War is as strong and as adequate as ever.

Our constitutional system for developing and carrying out our foreign policy rightly requires the cooperation of the President and of Congress, and the full understanding of the people. To my way of thinking, no nation, and surely no democratic nation, can carry out a sustained policy of any importance, especially one that may involve the catastro-phe of war, unless public opinion understands and accepts it. In any event, that should be our rule. It is our nature to abhor secret and unknown policies, carried out by stealth and manipulation. This is not to deny or to belittle the proper role of secrecy and privacy in negotiation. Diplomacy must often be discreet. But foreign policy is a different matter. Like all other policy, it should be subject to democratic control.

For twenty years, between 1947 and 1967—the period dominated by the Truman-Acheson foreign policy George Kennan helped to formulate—the United States had an effective and far-reaching foreign policy fully supported by an articulate and well-informed public opinion. What Kennan regards as our excessively democratic Constitution did not prevent the fulfillment of that policy. On the contrary, it made its success possible.

No branch of policy, however technical, is beyond the reach of the informed good sense of the American people. In my experience and study, the recent failures of American foreign policy were caused not by an excess of democracy, as Kennan contends, but by two quite different factors: by defects in our educational system, which result in a shaky and confused outlook about the purposes of foreign policy, and by widespread lapses from standards of responsibility. During the last decade, many who participated in the development of public opinion breached the basic rules of democratic ethics in failing to insist on the unpopular truth in their explanations of policy. When high officials are afraid to tell the American people the unvarnished truth, as they confront it in their daily work; when they tell the people untruths, or half-truths, hoping to soothe and manipulate opinion, and slip by at the next election; when they struggle to survive, rather than to do their duty; and when those who write and speak on these subjects follow their example, the constitutional process becomes diseased. Under these circumstances, it cannot produce sound policy.

In my view, the problems of democratic policymaking in the realm of foreign affairs are not structural. They cannot be cured by procedural changes, or by a shift of authority between Congress and the President, but only by more general adherence to the principles of discipline and candor in the process through which public opinion is crystallized from public debate. When debate is corrupted by fear, ignorance, or intellectual confusion, and when leaders are afraid to lead, policy is doomed to failure.

As I have suggested, it is only fair to appreciate Kennan's reflections on foreign policy as poetry. But they are also contributions of prestige and influence to the ongoing national debate that is shaping and reshaping our foreign policy. As such, they must be judged by the prosaic standards of ordinary reason: What assumptions is Kennan making? What set of propositions about the goals of our foreign policy is he using as the basis for his analysis? What is the relationship between the evidence and the deductions he draws from the propositions he treats as axiomatic? Despite the disjointed character of the book, the effort must be made, because Kennan is important.

The Shape of 'The Cloud'

The Cloud of Danger, its author tells us, is his first attempt to pull together his views on different aspects of American foreign policy and "to distill out of them something resembling a grand design of American foreign policy." Unfortunately, the book does not contain anything resembling a clear and systematic exposition of the goals and methods of American foreign policy—a statement of what it is for. Instead, one is left to piece together Kennan's presuppositions by examining scattered fragments.

The Cloud of Danger consists in the main of a travelogue—a series of comments, some casual, some sophisticated, about one region of the world after another. Those comments presuppose a definition of the national interest. But no definition is ever put forward as an analytical tool. Kennan's method gives the book a static quality. It is rare for Kennan to call his readers' attention to the fact that the political and strategic significance of many regions depends entirely on context, and that none can be excluded a priori from the purview of our concern. A few great centers of power are of obvious geopolitical importance in themselves: a shift of Western Europe, Japan, or China to Soviet control would totally alter the problem of American security. The fate of most other countries may or may not affect the national interests of the United States, depending upon circumstance. In terms of Kennan's analysis, for example, the withdrawal of Britain from Aden would be a matter of little concern to the United States; that would hardly be the case, however, even in Kennan's view, if Aden became a base for hostile operations against oil supplies for the Western Allies and Japan.

Kennan treats our interest in Japan and in Western Europe as of critical strategic importance to the security of the United States. He writes of Japan:

There can be no question but that the cornerstone of American policy in the Far East should be Japan.

. . . .

Japan . . . is *the* great industrial workshop of the Far East. Nothing else now in existence there compares with it. It is the only place where all the sinews of modern armed strength, from the most elementary to the most sophisticated, can be produced, if necessary, on short order. Should this potential come under the control of, or into close association with, one of the two great Communist landpowers, there is no predicting what uses might be made of it, and no certainty at all that these would be ones conducive to our security. So long as there prevails a relationship of mutual confidence, of community of aims, and of loyal collaboration between the Japanese and ourselves, we can be sure that this great hive of industrial and commercial activity will be a force for peace. Left to themselves, the Japanese, to avoid total isolation, would have to give a wholly different value to their relations with their great mainland neighbors; and we could never be sure where these new relationships would find their ending.

Does this passage mean that Kennan regards our security interest in Japan as what he would call "vital"—that is, worth fighting for in the event that the independence of Japan were threatened either by China or by the Soviet Union? He never uses the talismanic word. In Kennan's earlier mood of political realism, the answer would certainly be "Yes." But when Kennan is in the mood that dominates a large part of *The Cloud of Danger*, his answer to the question remains uncertain.

For example, Kennan recommends the withdrawal of our forces from South Korea and, implicitly, the termination of our security treaty with that country. Kennan contrasts the present situation in the Far East with that in 1950, when he argues that we were right to intervene. Now, he thinks, we could withdraw without creating the risk of crisis and trouble "in the surrounding region"—that is, in Japan, Taiwan, China, the Soviet Union, the other nations of the area, and the relations of all those countries with each other and with the United States. But a few pages earlier, Kennan wrote with force that we should defend our relationship with Japan because it would alter the balance of power if Japan fell under the control of either China or the Soviet Union—and then we could not tell what might happen. Kennan never explains how Japan could be protected if South Korea should be taken over by North Korea with Soviet help. Nor does he comment on what would happen to the political stability of the world, which depends upon the deterrent influence of American treaties and other commitments, if we should tear up a security treaty because the situation in the treaty area has become ominous. The other parties to such treaties can be forgiven for assuming that the treaties were adopted primarily to prevent war in ominous situations.

Kennan's analysis of the American security interest in Western Europe parallels his analysis of our relationship with Japan, but differs in method. With regard to Europe, Kennan is not concerned with the geopolitical balance of power, but with nearly pure sentimentality. He would drop Turkey, Greece, and Italy from NATO, but reaffirm the Treaty for the nations that he identifies as "our Western European friends." For all the friction between us and Western Europe, Kennan argues:

> [T]hese people are, for the most part, our best friends, almost our only friends—not in the sense that they like us, individually or collectively, but in the sense that they know us well, after so many mutual involvements; that they are aware, as are few others in this world, of their stake in the existence and the prospering (spiritually as well as economically) of our society; that they are conscious, in other words, of the community of fate that binds us all together and makes inconceivable, or difficult of conception, a promising future of the one without the other.

Of course, he says, the Western Europeans have a neurotic and childish fear that the Soviet Union would invade Western Europe unless strong NATO forces backed by the strategic and conventional power of the United States are on guard. European anxiety on this score, Kennan says, is a phantom, but

> we have no choice but to indulge it. In this respect, we have to treat our European friends as a species of psychiatric patient with hallucinations. . . .
> This means, of course, that the American military presence in Western Europe cannot be diminished. On the contrary, it should, in its conventional aspects, be increased, unless some real progress can be made in the Mutual and Balanced Force Reduction talks.

Here again, the contradictions and nonsequiturs in Kennan's reasoning are breathtaking. If there is no danger of a Soviet attack on Western Europe, as he argues, and no significance in the Soviet belief that visible military superiority would enable the Soviet Union to determine the course of world political development, then why should the NATO powers increase their forces in and near Europe?

Save by implication, the book contains no answer to these questions. Kennan never considers the question how Western Europe could be defended once we had withdrawn from the Mediterranean, the Near East, Greece, Turkey, and Africa, as he recommends. Nor does he set out the reasons why he supports a broad general policy of maintaining a position of deterrent military parity with the Soviet Union, both in strategic and in conventional forces. If he really believed that the foreign policy of the Soviet Union is defensive and pacific; that there is no danger of a Soviet invasion of Western Europe or even of Yugoslavia; and that we can have no interests worth worrying about in other parts of the world, including Greece, Italy, Turkey, and Israel, why does he say that our relations with the Soviet Union are the most important problem of our foreign policy, and that it is necessary for us to maintain a general position of military equality with that country? And why does he say, with regard to Japan, that we dare not allow Japan to fall under the control of China or the Soviet Union?

What emerges from reading *The Cloud of Danger* is the realization that its recommendations are drawn from two incompatible theories about the nature of modern international politics, theories that he never attempts either to articulate or to reconcile.

The first theory is explicit, or nearly explicit, and is the source for the most clearly stated aspects of Kennan's book. It is the nineteenth-century view that the United States can protect its political independence, territorial integrity, and prosperity by remaining neutral and apart, unless great convulsions should occur. The necessary predicate for this policy is the belief that the system itself will maintain minimal conditions of world public order. Thus, he urges, we should withdraw from Latin America, Africa, South Eastern Asia, and the Mediterranean basin without concern because we know that the system will maintain its equilibrium as it did in the nineteenth century, when world stability was organized by the European imperial system, and the Concert of Europe minimized the frictions of world politics. Those who believe that the Soviet Union is determined to enlarge its sphere of influence indefinitely by taking over the imperial positions of Great Britain and France are childish victims of paranoid nightmares, Kennan says, who know nothing of modern history, the Russian culture, or the nature of Soviet Communism.

The second theory on which Kennan's book is founded is exactly the opposite. We must at all times balance the military power of the Soviet Union because we cannot be sure what it would do if it achieved military superiority and began to change the balance of power in its favor. It is of course difficult to determine what the real military needs of the United States are. But such "real" needs do exist. And whatever they turn out to be, they must be met. However benign the intentions of the present generation of Soviet leaders may be, the essential lesson of all history is that the security of a nation depends on the maintenance of a balance of power, so that a potential adversary will not be tempted to strike for hegemony when he thinks circumstances are favorable.

Kennan uses two versions of classic balance of power theory in his analysis. The first is an extremely narrow definition of the true national interests of the United States in world society, based on the conviction that our genuinely vital interests should be defended by siege or fortress military methods, like those of the ill-fated Maginot Line. In Kennan's opinion, our safety as a nation requires us to maintain only the independence and political alignment of Northwestern Europe and Japan. Kennan is convinced that this goal can be achieved by withdrawing our presence and active concern from all other areas of the world, and relying on a much smaller military force to deter and if necessary defeat possible attacks directed against those interests. Military force capable of these missions is required, he believes, despite the fact that he also believes the Soviet Union is incapable of aggression and arms only for defense.

Kennan's second version of his attempt to define the American national interest in balance of power terms appears in *The Cloud of Danger* almost as a conditioned reflex. It is never explained. The lack of exposition is regrettable, for the concept is basic to his recommendation for maintaining a global military balance with the Soviet Union, and to other important passages in the book, notably his ideas about the Sino-Soviet conflict. In this perspective—that of classical balance of power analysis—Kennan would have to acknowledge that no area of the world can be considered to be outside the range of our interests, since any area of the world may become part of a process involving fundamental change in the balance of power. South Korea, Taiwan, or the Philippines may be used as stages in a campaign to gain control of China or Japan, as Africa and the Middle East may be invested to outflank Western Europe, and bring it under hegemonic control. Kennan advances this kind of reasoning to justify Western intervention in 1950 to protect South Korea against aggression, although he says that conditions have now changed so much that the United States can safely withdraw.

Kennan does not approach the problem as he did in *American Diplo-*

macy, 1900-1950, and in other early books and articles. In *American Diplomacy*, for example, he called attention to the deficiencies of America's understanding of her own relationship to the rest of the globe.

> [W] e can understand that we have had a stake in the prosperity and independence of the peripheral powers of Europe and Asia: those countries whose gazes were oriented outward, across the seas, rather than inward to the conquest of power on land.
>
> Now we see these things, or think we see them. But they were scarcely yet visible to the Americans of 1898, for those Americans had forgotten a great deal that had been known to their forefathers of a hundred years before. They had become so accustomed to their security that they had forgotten that it had any foundations at all outside our continent. They mistook our sheltered position behind the British fleet and British Continental diplomacy for the results of superior American wisdom and virtue in refraining from interfering in the sordid differences of the Old World. And they were oblivious to the first portents of the changes that were destined to shatter that pattern of security in the course of the ensuing half-century.

Save by remote implication, there is no trace of this view in *The Cloud of Danger*, although it is the basis for what I have identified here as the second of the theories of the national interest that animate Kennan's book, and indeed of the first as well.

The effort to isolate the essence of Kennan's thought, then, results in a series of unresolved contradictions. If one considers his arguments as dialectic exercises, they contain theses and antitheses, but no syntheses. The Soviet Union is and is not the most important problem we face in our foreign policy. It is expansionist, imperialist, and aggressive; it is defensive, cautious, and concerned only with its borders and their marches. The Cold War started with the Bolshevik Revolution, and never changes; the "détente" policy of Nixon and Kissinger, while oversold, did accomplish something, although Kennan never tells us what it was. The atoms of world politics constitute a system stable enough to function without our help, so that we can safely abstain from an active role in world affairs; as a result of two world wars and the rise of the Soviet Union, the world order of the nineteenth century is gone, and no new order based on rules acceptable to us can be brought into being unless we and our allies play a vigorous and sustained role in creating it.

The result of all these contradictions, and of the underlying ambiguity that gives rise to them, is that Kennan fails to give sufficient weight to the single greatest danger facing the United States today—the ever-increasing military power of the Soviet Union. As the Committee on the Present Danger has pointed out, the Soviet Union has been arming more rapidly than the United States and its allies. If present trends continue, we shall soon be in a position of strategic and conventional force inferiority, and therefore exposed not only to war but also to political coercion based on the credible threat of war.

Kennan does not tell us why the Soviet Union is arming so rapidly, and seeking to consolidate positions of strategic importance formerly occupied as imperial outposts by Great Britain, France, and Portugal. In a speech delivered since *The Cloud of Danger* was published—a speech that complements and clarifies some aspects of the book—Kennan argues that in order to make policy rationally we must examine the data about internal developments within the Soviet Union without regard to its military strength or its imperial policies. Kennan's proposal for a reasoned and courteous dialogue about the realities of Soviet policy is welcome, and important. But his astonishing suggestion—that the military aspects of the problem be, in effect, kept off the agenda—represents a considerable change from the position taken in *The Cloud of Danger*. In that book he seeks to explain and justify the Soviet military buildup as defensive, and to interpret the statistics in various reassuring patterns. But he does not challenge the fundamental thesis of those whose argument he is contesting—that the extraordinary and continuing increase of Soviet military strength during the last fifteen years, coupled with its policies of world-wide political expansion based on that military buildup, constitutes a threat to the security of the United States, a "present danger," in the phrase used by The Committee on the Present Danger, whose statements Kennan debates in his book. In *The Cloud of Danger*, Kennan says that the Committee is wrong in accepting exaggerated estimates of Soviet strength, and taking an alarmist view of Soviet intentions, but he basically agrees that the problem is real, and must be faced.

Hoping for a Miracle

It is difficult to conclude that the proposal made in Kennan's recent speech—put the problem of military balance aside—represents a fundamental change of view. The whole corpus of Kennan's work is based on a perspective that fully accepts the importance of power in world politics—sometimes reluctantly, but nonetheless firmly. One might interpret his suggestion, therefore, as representing a rather desperate hope for a miracle, a *deus ex machina*—the hope that economic troubles, demographic trends, or political change within the Soviet Union will bring about a reversal of the ominous trends measured by the statistics about the growth of Soviet military power, both strategic and conventional, and by the record of its recent behavior in Asia, Africa, and the Near East.

Kennan's argument on this point is central to his book. And it is profoundly wrong. American policy today, Kennan contends, faces a choice between two policies—one of peace, the other of war. The road to peace is the road of agreement with the Soviet Union. The road to war is the road of military buildup. If we move to maintain the military balance with the Soviet Union, enlarging our own military in order to keep up with the Soviet military programs, the result will surely be "a total militarization of policy and an ultimate showdown on the basis of armed strength." With great eloquence, Kennan therefore advocates agreements with the Soviets *without regard to the military balance*.

It has suddenly become fashionable in the United States, and in high circles of the government, to view the future course of American policy as Kennan does—as a simple choice between peace and war. But there is no such choice. Agreement with the Soviet Union and military equilibrium are not contradictory purposes, or alternative goals of policy. On the contrary, the obvious lesson of our whole experience with the Soviet Union is that there is no chance for a political agreement unless it is firmly based on deterrent military power. Kennan has always resisted and occasionally denied the political influence of military power. But it would be utopian, especially with regard to the Soviet Union, to pretend that military power is not an essential component of the process of history. Statements from the highest and most authoritative Soviet spokesmen in recent years have no room for doubt of the linkage between the Soviet Union's military buildup and the goal of "visible superiority," which in their view will determine the future course of international politics. Soviet behavior corresponds to that view of their policy.

No matter how conservatively those figures are evaluated, it is becoming more and more apparent that the pattern described by The Committee on the Present Danger is basically correct: the Soviet Union *is* increasing its military power in all categories far more rapidly than the United States; if present trends continue, the United States *will* confront the pressures of Soviet policy from a position of military inferiority. Given the expansionist pattern of Soviet policy, that would be a decidedly uncomfortable position, to put it mildly, and we ought to exert ourselves quickly to restore our deterrent capacities. Both the Brookings Institute and *Foreign Affairs* appear to have reached the same conclusion.

In effect, Kennan is asking the United States to ignore what the Soviet Union is doing, and the explanations for that policy offered by its highest and most responsible leaders, and to base our policy on his assurance that Mr. Brezhnev is a man of peace. That is an imprudent footing for national policy. If it should turn out that Mr. Kennan is in error, as The Committee on the Present Danger has said, "our alliances will weaken, [and] our promising rapprochement with China could be reversed. Then we could find ourselves isolated in a hostile world, facing the unremitting pressures of Soviet policy backed by an over-whelming preponderance of power. Our national survival itself would be in peril, and we should face, one after another, bitter choices between war and acquiescence under pressure."

The Cost of Shortsightedness

Reflecting on the factors that have brought British power to an end, Correlli Barnett asks

> *why* such a particular stamp of men as Baldwin and MacDonald, Chamber-lain, Simon and Halifax, Henderson and Eden, held sway in British politics between the wars; *why* British public opinion was so pacifistic and interna-tionalist; *why* 'appeasement' was so widely congenial and re-armament so repugnant; *why* British governments handled international crises in the feeble and nerveless way they did; *why* the British permitted the catastrophic decline of their industrial power; *why* the Empire was allowed to remain a source of strategic weakness and danger.

Barnett comments that something in the British character, and in the educational system and the political atmosphere of Britain, then and now, kept that country from facing the facts, and dealing with them in time. Because Britain failed to pursue the resolute and clearsighted policy that might have prevented the two World Wars of this century, it has ceased to be a major influence in world politics, despite its heroism on the battlefield. The theme of the final volume of Churchill's memoir of the Second World War is "How the Great Democracies Triumphed, and so Were able to Resume the Follies Which Had so Nearly Cost Them Their Life."

At incalculable cost, the world has endured two convulsive World Wars that wise and vigorous British statesmanship could have prevented. In my view, the wars could never have occurred if, in 1905, the British had entered into a full and visible military alliance with France, and adopted conscription, or if Britain and France had occupied the Rhineland in 1936, or even if they had reacted firmly to the German takeover of the Sudetenland in 1938.

The two World Wars transformed the world. They permitted Communist parties to seize power in Russia and China while those countries suffered the anarchy of defeat. They released the terrible demons in the human spirit that made Mussolini and Hitler possible, and so many other tyrants, too. And they forced us at last to emerge from the cocoon of our nineteenth-century isolation and neutrality.

We share many of the impulses and yearnings of the British view of world politics, as *The Cloud of Danger* attests. But we are not as well off as Britain was in 1913 or 1938. No matter how badly Britain conducted its affairs, the American giant always loomed in the wings, able to protect Britain against the ultimate consequences of its folly. There is no sleeping giant to save us from our folly, if we persist in the course Mr. Kennan defends with such passion in *The Cloud of Danger*.

PART THREE

In addition to the question of the merits of Kennan's recent views there is the question of whether they represent a departure from those he held during the period when he helped to formulate major American foreign policies, or whether the body of his beliefs is internally consistent and has been consistent over time.

Two scholars debate this problem, each armed with a formidable array of historical reference material. Although the debate did not conclude with these two articles, the selections in Part Three contain the essentials. Readers wishing to follow the further developments are referred to subsequent issues of *Foreign Affairs*.

11. Mr. "X" Is Consistent and Right

John Lewis Gaddis

Two questions are debated here: Were Kennan's original views on containment really what he later claimed them to be? What were the implications of these views when he first enunciated them?

John Lewis Gaddis, Professor of History at Ohio University in Athens, Ohio, comes down on the side of Mr. Kennan's own reinterpretation of what his containment ideas in the original "X" article were supposed to mean. According to Kennan and Gaddis, the Soviet Union was to be contained primarily by political, as opposed to military, means. Further, the policy was applicable only to the industrialized states of Europe and Japan. Gaddis also agrees with Kennan that Kennan's views were widely misunderstood and that the policies actually pursued by Washington were, for the most part, contrary to his advice.

Reprinted by permission from *Foreign Affairs*, July 1977; the article appeared there under the title "Containment: A Reassessment." Copyright 1977 by Council on Foreign Relations, Inc.

"I FELT LIKE ONE WHO HAS inadvertently loosened a large boulder from the top of a cliff and now helplessly witnesses its path of destruction in the valley below, shuddering and wincing at each successive glimpse of disaster."[1] So George F. Kennan described the consequences of having published in this journal, 30 years ago this month, the article which introduced the term "containment" to the world. Attributed only to a "Mr. X" in order to protect the author's position as Director of the State Department's new Policy Planning Staff, the article, entitled "The Sources of Soviet Conduct," was nonetheless quickly revealed by Arthur Krock as having come from Kennan's pen. Ironically, its very anonymity assured it a conspicuousness Kennan's subsequent efforts to clarify his views never attained.

No article in the history of *Foreign Affairs* has been more frequently reprinted; none, it would also appear safe to say, has lent itself to more variant interpretations. "Containment" has been defined as a global commitment to resist communism everywhere; as a passive, negative condemnation of millions to enslavement behind the iron curtain; as a blueprint for the domination of the world by American imperialism, and as the short-sighted acquiescence of a dutiful giant in the process of being nibbled away by midgets. Its critics have ranged from Robert A. Taft and John Foster Dulles to Walter Lippmann and J. William Fulbright; it has been invoked to justify such diverse enterprises as the Marshall Plan, NATO, the Korean "police action," the Eisenhower Doctrine, and, to its inventor's most intense discomfort, the war in Vietnam.

Historians have argued for years over what Kennan meant to say in the "X" article, and Kennan himself has attempted to resolve this issue in his *Memoirs*. But recollections are, of necessity, selective; critics have charged as well that elements of self-justification entered into Kennan's account.[2] Within the past few years, however, thanks to the declassification of National Security Council and Policy Planning Staff documents from the 1947-1949 period and the partial opening of the Kennan Papers, it has become possible to compare what Kennan said publicly and in his *Memoirs* with the positions he was taking inside the government at the time. These sources confirm Kennan's assertion that the "X" article was an incomplete and misleading reflection of his views. They also suggest that "containment," properly understood, is by no means an outmoded concept; that aspects of it bear striking relevance to problems the Carter Administration is likely to confront as it enters the fourth decade of what we may still regard, with some qualifications, as the cold war.

The Paradoxes of 'X'

One of several paradoxes associated with the "X" article is that it was taken at the time, and continues to be remembered, as a work of prescription. Such was not its primary emphasis. Rather, Kennan devoted most of the piece to an explanation of Soviet hostility toward the West. Of the article's 17 pages, only three contained what might be considered recommendations for action by the United States, and these were couched only in general terms. For a document hailed as providing a new strategic concept for the postwar world, the "X" article in fact said remarkably little about strategy.

Kennan attributed Soviet hostility to a deep and brooding sense of uneasiness on the part of Kremlin leaders. This phenomenon reflected, to some extent, historical experience: lacking protective geographical barriers and subject, throughout its history, to recurrent invasion, the Russian state had never enjoyed the luxury of free security Americans had always taken for granted. Partly, the tendency arose also out of the conspiratorial habits formed by Bolshevik organizers during years in the underground: survival, for them, had come to depend on trusting no one. It was these two forms of insecurity—historical and organizational—which accounted for the peculiar and difficult behavior of the Soviet Union under Josef Stalin.

Ideology, in Kennan's scheme of things, performed several functions. It served to legitimize an illegitimate regime: if one could not claim to rule by the will of God, as had the Russian tsars, then ruling by the will of history, in the form of the Marxian dialectic, was the next best thing. It also provided justification for the repression without which Soviet leaders, unimaginative as they were, did not know how to rule: as long as most of the world was capitalist, harsh measures could be portrayed as necessary to protect the leading communist state. Finally, ideology was significant because it associated the Soviet Union with revolutionary aspirants in other countries, thus giving the Kremlin, through the international communist movement, an instrument with which to project influence beyond its borders.

But Kennan did not see ideology as a determinant of Soviet policy. The body of doctrine which made up communism was so amorphous that it required an intermediary to relate and apply it to the real world. This circumstance placed that intermediary—the Soviet government— in a position to say what ideology was at any given moment. "The leadership is at liberty," Kennan wrote,

> to put forward for tactical purposes any particular thesis which it finds useful to the cause at any particular moment and to require the faithful and un- questioning acceptance of that thesis by the members of the movement as a whole. This means that truth is not a constant but is actually created, for all intents and purposes, by the Soviet leaders themselves. It may vary from week to week, from month to month. It is nothing absolute and immutable.

Communism, then, was not so much a guide to action as a justification for action already decided upon. It was true, Kennan implied, that Stalin might not feel secure until he had come to dominate the entire world, but that attitude grew out of the dictator's own unfathomable sense of insecurity, not out of any principled commitment to the goal of an international classless society.

Kennan regarded Soviet expansionism as both easier and more dif- ficult to deal with than that of Napoleon or Hitler: easier because it had no fixed timetable and would yield in the face of resistance; more difficult because of its persistence, its refusal to be discouraged by individual setbacks. It was within this context that Kennan made his call for a "long-term, patient but firm and vigilant containment of Rus- sian expansive tendencies." "Soviet pressure against the free institu- tions of the western world," he continued, "is something that can be contained by the adroit and vigilant application of counterforce at a series of constantly shifting geographical and political points, corre- sponding to the shifts and manoeuvres of Soviet policy."

Prospects for such an approach were favorable, Kennan maintained, because of the vulnerabilities which existed within Soviet society. These included the human costs of forced industrialization and terror, the destruction of war, the uneven nature of Soviet economic devel- opment, the problem of succession after Stalin's death, potential antag- onism between the Party leadership and its rank and file, and the pos- sibility that revolutionary movements outside the U.S.S.R. might look to places other than Moscow for inspiration and leadership. Kennan concluded this section of his article with a reference to the proposition, advanced in Thomas Mann's *Buddenbrooks,* that "human institutions often show the greatest outward brilliance at a moment when inner decay is in reality farthest advanced.''

Given these circumstances, the United States could not expect to enjoy political intimacy with the Soviet regime, but neither should it regard war as inevitable. Nor did it have to resign itself to an indefinite policy of ''holding the line and hoping for the best,'' for ''it is entirely possible for the United States to influence by its actions the internal developments, both within Russia and throughout the international Communist movement, by which Russian policy is largely determined.'' This could be done by its ''creat[ing] among the peoples of the world generally the impression of a country which knows what it wants, which is coping successfully with the problems of its internal life and with the responsibilities of a World Power, and which has a spiritual vitality capable of holding its own among the major ideological currents of the time.'' The result, in due course, would be ''either the break-up or the gradual mellowing of Soviet power,'' for the simple reason that ''no mystical, Messianic movement—and particularly not that of the Kremlin—can face frustration indefinitely without eventually adjusting itself in one way or another to the logic of that state of affairs.'' All that was needed, then, was for the United States to ''measure up to its own best traditions and prove itself worthy of preservation as a great nation.''

The Critics' Response

Such, in brief, was the substance of the ''X'' article. It is hardly necessary to dwell on the criticisms it provoked, first and most eloquently from Walter Lippmann, who dismissed containment as a ''strategic monstrosity,'' and then from a host of other commentators, on both the Right and the Left. Basically these complaints boiled down to three points: (1) that Kennan's determination ''to confront the Russians with unalterable counterforce at every point where they show signs of encroaching upon the interests of a peaceful and stable world'' would allow Moscow to determine the time, place, and nature of competition, and would as a consequence risk the commitment of American resources on unsuitable terrain; (2) that Kennan failed to make clear whether the roots of Soviet behavior were ideological or national, and so obscured the distinction between Russian expansionism and international communism; and (3) that by calling for actions which could only reinforce Stalin's paranoia, Kennan was precluding any movement toward the disengagement of Soviet and American forces in Europe, and an eventual negotiated settlement of outstanding differences.[3]

Certainly the first criticism was justified: Kennan's language did appear to imply relinquishing the strategic initiative to the Russians. Such a course of action would mean, Lippmann charged, that "for ten or fifteen years Moscow, not Washington, would define the issues, would make the challenges, would select the ground where the conflict was to be waged, and would choose the weapons." Containment could only be implemented "by recruiting, subsidizing and supporting a heterogeneous array of satellites, clients, dependents and puppets, . . . a coalition of disorganized, disunited, feeble or disorderly nations, tribes, and factions around the perimeter of the Soviet Union."

In fact, though, such lack of discrimination in defining interests and choosing allies was the last thing Kennan favored. We know from Joseph Jones' book that he opposed the sweeping language of the Truman Doctrine; the first Policy Planning Staff paper, written in May 1947, advised taking steps to correct the impression that "the Truman Doctrine is a blank check to give economic and military aid to any area in the world where the Communists show signs of being successful." "It may be that we have undertaken too much," Kennan admitted to a National War College audience the following month; "there is a serious gap . . . between the things we have set out to do and our capabilities for doing them." Another Policy Planning Staff paper, completed in July, noted that "the extent of the calls on this country is so great in relation to our resources that we could not contemplate assistance to others on any universal basis, even if this were desirable. A beginning would have to be made somewhere, and the best place for a beginning is obviously in Europe."[4]

Kennan's emphasis on limited means, and on the consequent need to differentiate interests, comes through clearly in a comprehensive "Resumé of [the] World Situation" which he prepared for Secretary of State George C. Marshall in November 1947. The effort to stop the Soviet Union's political advance had "stretched our resources dangerously far in several respects," he argued; "it is clearly unwise for us to continue the attempt to carry alone, or largely single-handed, the opposition to Soviet expansion. It is urgently necessary for us to restore something of the balance of power in Europe and Asia by strengthening local forces of independence and by getting them to assume part of the burden." Significantly, Kennan described the European Recovery Program, then just getting underway, as "probably . . . the last major effort of this nature which our people could, or should, make."[5]

Kennan held out little hope for American interests in the Far East, not because that region was unimportant, but because the United States lacked the capacity to affect events there in any decisive way. "It is urgently necessary," he wrote in February 1948, "that we recognize our own limitations as a moral and ideological force among the Asiatic peoples." After conversations with General Douglas MacArthur in Tokyo in March, Kennan expressed support for a "political-strategic concept" based on the notion that "while we would endeavor to influence events on the mainland of Asia in ways favorable to our security, we would not regard any mainland areas as vital to us." Such an approach meant, in Kennan's view, no further involvement in the Chinese civil war, the gradual withdrawal of U.S. forces from South Korea, the demilitarization and neutralization of Japan and the Philippines, and the maintenance of American bases on Okinawa, Guam, and the former Japanese-mandated islands.[6]

"Repeatedly," Kennan wrote in his *Memoirs*, "I expressed in talks and lectures the view that there were only five regions of the world— the United States, the United Kingdom, the Rhine valley with adjacent industrial areas, the Soviet Union, and Japan—where the sinews of modern military strength could be produced in quantity; I pointed out that only one of these was under Communist control; and I defined the main task of containment, accordingly, as one of seeing to it that none of the remaining ones fell under such control."[7] The documents now available leave little doubt that this was, in fact, Kennan's view at the time.[8] One can only marvel, as Kennan does in his *Memoirs*, at the extent to which the "X" article managed to convey precisely the opposite impression.

The confusion arose largely out of Kennan's failure to explain what he meant by "counterforce." Without further qualification the word suggested, and was taken by Lippmann to mean, military resistance to Soviet expansion wherever it occurred. But a preliminary version of the "X" article, found in the Kennan Papers, conveys a very different impression. The passage is worth quoting in full:

> The problem of meeting the Kremlin in international affairs therefore boils down to this: Its inherent expansive tendencies must be firmly contained at all times by counter-pressure which makes it constantly evident that attempts

to break through this containment would be detrimental to *Soviet* interests. The irritating by-products of an ideology indispensable to the Soviet regime for internal reasons must not be allowed to become the cause of hysterical alarm or of tragic despair among those abroad who are working towards a happier association of the Russian people with the world community of nations. The United States, in particular, must demonstrate by its own self-confidence and patience, but particularly by the integrity and dignity of its example, that the true glory of the Russian national effort can find its expression only in peaceful association with other peoples and not in attempts to subjugate and dominate those peoples. Such an attitude on the part of this country would have with it the deepest logic of history; and in the long run it could not fail to carry conviction and to find reflection in the development of Russia's internal political life and, accordingly, in the Soviet concept of Russia's place in international affairs.[9]

One need hardly emphasize the difference between this passage, which describes "counter-pressure" as an effort to encourage, by example, long-term changes in the Soviet concept of international relations, and the "X" article's apparent endorsement of "counterforce," to be applied in circumstances which the Russians could largely control. It is a startling demonstration of the misunderstandings which can flow from a slight shift of phrase, combined with an excessive devotion to the principle of economy in prose.

A second point on which the "X" article was misunderstood had to do with the question of what was to be contained: Soviet expansionism or international communism. Lippmann accused Kennan of having become "exclusively preoccupied with Marxian ideology, and with the communist revolution." "It was the mighty power of the Red Army, not the ideology of Karl Marx, which enabled the Russian government to expand its frontiers," Lippmann pointed out; "the policy which I suggest is . . . to divide the Red Army from the Red International."[10]

It is true that Kennan, like most observers at the time, used the terms "communism" and "Soviet expansionism" almost interchangeably. But a careful reading of the "X" article would hardly sustain the argument that is was "exclusively preoccupied" with ideology; rather, as noted earlier, it emphasized the malleable nature of communism and the extent to which ideology reflected Soviet national interests. "The role of ideology in Soviet political society, while of tremendous importance, is not primarily that of a basic determinant of political action," Kennan wrote in his preliminary version of the "X" article. "It is rather a prism through which Soviet eyes must view the world, and an indispensable vehicle for the translation into words and actions of impulses and aspirations which have their origin deeper still. . . . But it is important to remember that its bearing is on coloration of background, on form of expression, and on method of execution, rather than on basic aim."[11]

Kennan drew from this the conclusion that a communist regime beyond the reach of Soviet military or police power would pose no great threat to American security, and might even offer certain advantages. As he explained at the University of Virginia in February 1947:

> Perhaps this bubble cannot really be pricked until one of these parties has come into power in a country not contiguous to the borders of the direct military power of Russia. . . . A communist regime in power in some such country which either failed to meet its responsibilities and discredited itself in the eyes of the people or which turned on its masters, repudiated the Kremlin's authority, and bit the hand that had reared it, might be more favorable to the interests of this country and of world peace in the long run than an unscrupulous opposition party spewing slander from the safe vantage point of irresponsibility.

Kennan went on to predict in this lecture that if the Chinese Communists ever gained control in China, "the men in the Kremlin would suddenly discover that this fluid subtle oriental movement which they thought they held in the palm of their hand had quietly oozed away between their fingers and that there was nothing left there but a ceremonious Chinese bow and a polite and inscrutable Chinese giggle."[12]

The idea of encouraging tension between the Soviet Union and the international communist movement lay behind several of Kennan's most important policy recommendations during this period. His suggestion, in the summer of 1947, that Marshall Plan aid be offered to the Soviet Union and its East European satellites was an attempt, not only to place the onus for dividing Europe on the Russians, but also to strain the relationship between the Kremlin and its clients. Early in 1948, he recommended relating the level of U.S. naval and air activity in the Eastern Mediterranean to the level of communist activity in Italy and Greece, with the thought that a conflict would thereby be produced between the interests of Greek and Italian Communists on the one hand, and Soviet security requirements on the other. "In conflicts of this sort," he noted, "the interests of narrow Soviet nationalism usually win."[13]

Given this background, it is hardly surprising that Kennan welcomed Tito's break with Moscow in the summer of 1948. As a Policy Planning Staff study noted in June:

> The international communist movement will never be able to make good entirely the damage done by this development. For the first time in the history of the movement, a servant of the international communist movement controlling territory, armed forces, and a political organization, has defied, with at least temporary success, the authority of the Kremlin. This example will be noted by other communists everywhere. Eventually, the non-Russian communists will come to appreciate that they have no future as servants of Kremlin policies.

Kennan cited a communist China as one country where Titoist tendencies might manifest themselves; so, too, were the remaining satellites in Eastern Europe. The first comprehensive National Security Council study on that part of the world, which originated as a Policy Planning Staff document and was approved by President Truman in December 1949, called for fostering "a heretical drifting-away process on the part of the satellite states." Such a trend might eventually result, it noted, in the formation of "two opposing blocs in the communist world," a situation which could "provide us with an opportunity to operate on the basis of a balance in the communist world, and to foster the tendencies toward accommodation with the West implicit in such a state of affairs."[14]

Behind this anticipation of polycentrism within the international communist movement was a simple confidence in the durability of nationalism, and in the Russians' chronic inability to avoid alienating those with whom they came in contact. "The actions of people in power are often controlled far more by the circumstances in which they are obliged to exercise that power than by the ideas and principles which animated them when they were in opposition," a Policy Planning Staff study concluded in August 1948. Moreover,

> Kremlim leaders are so over-bearing and so cynical in the discipline they impose on their followers that few can stand their authority for very long. . . . Conditions are therefore favorable to a concerted effort on our part designed to take advantage of Soviet mistakes and of the rifts that have appeared, and to promote the steady deterioration of the structure of moral influence by which the authority of the Kremlin has been carried to peoples far beyond the reach of Soviet police power.[15]

What these documents show, then, is that there was no contradiction between the concepts of "containment" and "liberation," if by that latter term is meant the cautious encouragement of centrifugal tendencies within the international communist movement. But it should be noted that this approach implied "liberation" only from Soviet control, not necessarily from communism. "We are not necessarily always against the expansion of communism, and certainly not always against it to the same degree in every area," Kennan observed late in 1947; "it all depends on circumstances."[16] If ideology reflected rather than determined state interests, it followed that communism posed a threat to American security only where linked to, and the reliable instrument of, a state like the Soviet Union, which combined hostility with the ability to do something about it.

The third major criticism which Lippmann made regarding the "X" article was that "the policy of containment . . . does not have as its objective a settlement of the conflict with Russia." Lippmann went on to urge the mutual withdrawal of "non-European" armies from Europe.[17] It is true that the "X" article made no specific proposals along these lines, although it did foresee, over an indeterminate length of time, a gradual "mellowing" of the Soviet regime which might make it possible to relax tensions. The documents show, though, that while Kennan was not sanguine about the prospects, he was prepared to explore opportunities for negotiations even before Stalin's death; that his own proposal for disengagement in Europe, which caused such a furor when broached publicly in the 1957 Reith lectures, had in fact been advanced tentatively within the government as early as 1948.

Kennan had always taken the position that negotiations required not so much strength as self-confidence. Military power had its uses, he acknowledged: "You have no idea how much it contributes to the general politeness and pleasantness of diplomacy when you have a little quiet armed force in the background." But the military balance alone would not determine the course of negotiations, simply because weapons and troop levels were only one of several components of power on the international scene. "Remember that . . . as things stand today," he told a National War College audience in October 1947, "it is not Russian military power which is threatening us, it is Russian political power. . . . If it is not entirely a military threat, I doubt that it can be effectively met entirely by military means." Kennan had concluded, by the end of 1947, that the psychological impact of the Marshall Plan had restored a substantial degree of self-confidence in Europe, and had provided "the greatest shock to Soviet foreign policy since the invasion of Russia by the Germans in 1941."[18] If those trends continued, he believed, the time would be right to begin investigating prospects for accommodation with Moscow.

In a February 1948 Policy Planning Staff paper, Kennan advocated preparations for negotiations with the Russians aimed at persuading them "(a) to reduce communist pressures elsewhere in Europe and the Middle East to a point where we can afford to withdraw all our armed forces from the continent and the Mediterranean; and (b) to acquiesce thereafter in a prolonged period of stability in Europe." "The day will come when the Russians will find it to their advantage to talk to us," Kennan wrote two months later in an unsent letter to Walter Lippmann, "and it may be sooner than many of us suspect. That day will come when they have arrived at the conclusion that they cannot have what they want *without* talking to us."[19]

Underlying Kennan's position was the assumption that the Soviet Union was not impervious to outside influences; that change was at least as inevitable there as in the West, and that, through careful diplomacy, such changes could be turned to the West's advantage. As a Policy Planning study put it:

> The Soviet leaders are prepared to recognize *situations*, if not arguments. If, therefore, situations can be created in which it is clearly not to the advantage of their power to emphasize the elements of conflict in their relations with the outside world, then their actions, and even the tenor of their propaganda to their own people, *can* be modified.[20]

It was this belief in the mutability of ideology, an idea Kennan had expressed clearly but to little effect in the "X" article, which formed the basis of his argument that Soviet hostility toward the outside world need not last forever, and that it was in the interests of the United States to be prepared to benefit from such modifications in the Russians' behavior as might arise.

Overall, though, the "X" article expressed Kennan's concept of containment in an inaccurate and incomplete manner. Kennan's admitted imprecision of language contributed to this misunderstanding, as did the fact that his official position precluded public clarification. Lippmann compounded the problem by focusing his objections on selected portions of the article, ignoring especially its broader implications regarding the role of ideology in the Soviet state. But whatever the causes of the original confusion, there is sufficient evidence in the newly released documents to corroborate Kennan's argument, made ten years ago in his *Memoirs*, that the "X" article should no longer be taken as the definitive statement of what he meant by "containment."[21]

Stages of Containment

"It was not 'containment' that failed," Kennan wrote in those *Memoirs;* "it was the intended follow-up that never occurred." There is, in fact, much to be said for viewing containment as a process involving several stages: first, restoration of a balance of power in areas threatened by Soviet expansionism; second, reduction of the Soviet Union's influence beyond its borders through the cautious exploitation of antagonisms between Moscow and the international communist movement; and third, as a long-range objective, alteration of the Soviet concept of international relations as a means of facilitating a negotiated settlement of outstanding differences.[22] Only the first of these stages can be said to have been fully implemented during the early years of the cold war; ironically, its very success impeded progress toward the other two.

The problem was the extent to which Kennan's strategy relied on psychology. He sought to deny key industrial areas to the Russians, but to do so primarily by instilling a sense of self-confidence in the minds of the people who lived there. That approach placed his program at the mercy of whatever fears, rational or irrational, those people might hold.

One such fear was the prospect of Soviet military attack, and the possibility that the United States might not be able to do anything about it. Kennan thought this fear groundless, but in the end he was forced to acknowledge that self-confidence in Western Europe would not develop without a specific security guarantee by the United States. Another concern was the possibility that German militarism might revive; that prospect made the indefinite partition of Germany more attractive to most West Europeans than reunification. The difficulty with such measures as the North Atlantic Treaty and the establishment of an independent West German state was that they tended to perpetuate the division of Europe into two hostile camps, thereby delaying the negotiations leading toward Soviet and American disengagement which Kennan thought essential for stability in that part of the world. Nor would it be easy to call a halt once the process of forming alliances had begun: "There is no logical stopping point in the development of a system of anti-Russian alliances," Kennan wrote late in 1948, "until that system has circled the globe and has embraced all the non-communist countries of Europe, Asia, and Africa."[23]

Another unanticipated difficulty involved the psychological effect communist victories in countries not vital to American security could have in those which were. It is significant that Kennan supported aid to Greece and Turkey in 1947, not because those states were on his list of key industrial regions which had to be kept out of Russian hands, but because of the impression their collapse would have produced in Western Europe, which was such a region. For similar reasons, he endorsed the decision to aid South Korea in 1950, even though three years earlier he had described the American position there as untenable, and had advocated withdrawal as soon as possible.[24] It was not all that difficult, then, to slide from a belief that the balance of power required nothing more than a limited application of effort in a few key locations to a conviction that that balance could be maintained only by massive expenditures of energy in peripheral areas.

Nor was it a simple matter to maintain the distinction between Soviet expansionism and international communism. Confusion on this point stemmed partly from the Truman Administration's imprecise public rhetoric: in order to get its foreign aid program through the Congress, the Administration had found it necessary to present the Soviet threat in global terms, an approach which did not encourage differentiation between varieties of communism. The heated political atmosphere of the period also caused problems: even before Senator Joseph R. McCarthy had given his name to the syndrome, expressions of willingness to deal with communists anywhere had begun to risk accusations of disloyalty, even treason. Reinforcing these tendencies was an increasingly widespread habit of using ideology as a predictive instrument, of assuming that ideological orientation took precedence over other influences in determining the behavior of states, and could be used as a basis upon which to anticipate their behavior. The combined effect of these trends was to inhibit further efforts to exploit differences within the international communist movement.

Yet another problem with Kennan's strategy was its emphasis on Soviet intentions rather than on capabilities; on what the Russians were likely to do, rather than on what they could do.[25] This was not an easy approach to sustain because it ran up against the national security bureaucracy's proclivity for worst-case analysis. It required accepting on faith the notion that the Russians did not want a war when in fact many of their actions—Czechoslovakia, Berlin, Korea—appeared to indicate the opposite. Kennan's emphasis on intentions became even harder to maintain once it had become clear that the Soviet Union had the potential, should war come, of inflicting substantial damage on the United States and its allies. News of the Russian atomic bomb made it appear much less risky to base military planning on Soviet capabilities rather than intentions; the price, though, was a persistent overestimation of Soviet strength, and an equally persistent lack of enthusiasm for negotiations until perceived strategic inadequacies had been remedied.

Finally, a fundamental assumption underlying Kennan's concept of containment had been the awareness that the United States lacked the resources to sustain worldwide commitments, and that, accordingly, hard choices would have to be made between what it would have to accept, and what it could reasonably expect to change. American officials never entirely lost sight of that fact, but the conclusions of the strategic reassessment which took place early in 1950—that means were capable of greater expansion than had been thought—had strong appeal; there ensued, as a result, a certain loss of sensitivity to the relationship between costs and commitments which Kennan had so strongly stressed.[26]

There was, in all of these problems, a common thread: all of them—preoccupation with building alliances, the use of ideology as a predictive instrument, concern with credibility, the emphasis on commitments and neglect of costs—reflect excessive attention to the processes of diplomacy, and a corresponding tendency to lose sight of objectives. They reflect an inclination to let strategy dictate policy rather than the other way around. To the extent that the United States contributed to the perpetuation of the cold war, it was in large part as a result of this confusion between ends and means, of the habit of concentrating so much on the mechanisms of containment as to lose sight of precisely what it was that strategy was supposed to contain.

But if Kennan's critics within the government preoccupied themselves excessively with processes, it must be noted that he himself leaned too far in the other direction by failing to devote sufficient attention to the problems of implementing containment. Skeptical of the efficacy of written policy statements as guides to action, Kennan relied simply on the continued presence of qualified experts to guide the hand of policymakers, much as he had done with Secretary of State Marshall between 1947 and 1949. He gave little thought to what might happen if those policymakers, or the bureaucracies they controlled, failed to seek such advice.[27] Nor did he concern himself adequately with the question of how self-confidence could be maintained, whether within the government, with the general public, or among allies overseas, while at the same time making the sharp distinctions between vital and peripheral interests, varieties of communism, and adversary capabilities and intentions upon which his strategy depended so heavily.

Partly because of this combination of difficulties (and partly also because of external circumstances), it would not be until the early 1970s that the United States would undertake a sustained effort to implement what Kennan had regarded as "the intended follow-up" to containment—the exploitation of fissures within the international communist movement, and the exploration with the Russians of opportunities for reducing tensions through negotiations. There is irony in the fact that these initiatives occurred during the administration of a President who, in his early career, had denounced Kennan's ideas as passive and defeatist. The diplomacy of Richard M. Nixon and Henry A. Kissinger was not so much a conceptual breakthrough, then, as it was a return to the unimplemented aspects of containment Kennan had proposed a quarter of a century before.

Sources of Stability

To a considerable degree, the original objectives of containment have now been achieved. Whether because of the nuclear weapons stalemate or the diffusion of power from large states to small, there exists today a more stable international equilibrium than most observers 30 years ago would have thought possible. Certainly a split has developed between the Soviet Union and the international communist movement: the word "communist" now takes in such a diversity of systems and personalities as to render it little more than a semantic expression. Nor can it be denied that changes have taken place in the way the Russians view the international order. There is room for debate over how far they have come in accommodating themselves to it, but there can be little question that "mellowing" has taken place since Stalin's day.

But these things have happened more in spite of than because of American policy. The United States did, of course, play a vital role in restoring the balance of power in Europe after World War II. By maintaining its end of the nuclear balance, it contributed further to that stability. But the other great force which has constrained the superpowers—the rise of nationalism—has proceeded for the most part independently of American efforts; by the early 1950s Washington officials had lost sight of Kennan's idea of working with nationalism to contain the Russians. Similarly, the American proclivity for employing ideology as a predictive instrument may well have delayed fragmentation of the communist monolith. It was no small feat to begin treating communism as a unit at precisely the moment, with the emergence of Tito in Yugoslavia and Mao in China, that it ceased to be one. Nor has the United States helped all that much in smoothing the Kremlin's path toward a new view of the international order. By refraining for so long from negotiating with the Russians, we very likely confirmed their fears of the outside world; more recently, in the view of some, we have negotiated too often, thereby encouraging Moscow to take the outside world too much for granted.

There is need to align American policies, to a greater extent than has been done in the recent past, with what is already happening in the world—to let events work for us, rather than against us. Kennan argued 30 years ago that the United States could more easily find security in a diverse world than could the Russians. There is no reason to think that any less true today. Possibly there should be a new name for this strategy: "containment" always was something of a misnomer, suggesting as it did the disconcerting precedents of Sisyphus, or the boy with a finger in the dike. But whatever the label, the assumption behind Kennan's argument in this respect remains valid—that the United States can tolerate diversity with greater self-confidence than can the Soviet Union, and that, as a consequence, the overall "correlation of forces" in the world need not be regarded as necessarily inimical to our interests.

There are other ways in which Kennan's ideas from the 1940s might be fruitfully applied to contemporary affairs. One would be to stop using ideology as a predictive instrument. It would be helpful to recognize that we have been no more successful in anticipating the behavior of communist states on the basis of their ideological orientation than they have been in anticipating our own. Compared to such entrenched phenomena as nationalism, racism, greed, or sheer human intractability, communism is today a relatively insignificant determinant of events on the international scene, unless of course we choose to impart significance to it by giving it more attention than it deserves. The objective of containment was, and still should be, to limit the expansion of Soviet influence in the world. To allow energies and resources to be diverted to the task of opposing something called "international communism" is not only to pervert the intent of Kennan's strategy; it is to embark in pursuit of a phantom.

We can also learn from Kennan a certain skepticism regarding the dangers posed by Soviet hegemonic aspirations. Because the Russians handle diversity badly, their attempts to expand influence tend to take on anti-national characteristics, and to generate in time their own resistance. "One must not be too frightened," Kennan observed in his *Memoirs*,

> of those who aspire to world domination. No one people is great enough to establish a world hegemony. There are built-in impediments to the permanent exertion by any power of dominant influence in areas which it is unable to garrison and police, or at least to overshadow from positions of close proximity, by its own troops. [28]

This is nothing more than a recognition of the "staying power" of nationalism, and of the inescapable effects of what Clausewitz a century and a half ago called "friction." (The principle is known to a more recent generation of strategists as Murphy's Law: "What can go wrong will go wrong.") One can always question such reassurances from "worst-case" perspectives, but the phenomenon they describe has rarely failed to manifest itself.

Similarly, it would be advantageous to keep in mind Kennan's admonition that there should be some correspondence, in strategy, between the effect desired and that likely to be produced. "The world situation is not something which exists independently of our defense policy and to which we need only react," Kennan wrote in 1948. "It will be deeply influenced by the measures which we ourselves take. . . . Our policies must therefore be viewed not only as a means of reacting to a given situation, but as a means of influencing a situation as well." [29] It is all too easy, in concentrating on an assessment of adversary capabilities and intentions, to forget the extent to which they are apt to be the product of one's own.

Finally, there is in Kennan's approach a set of propositions so obvious that they often escape notice: that there are limits to power; that there are no commitments without costs; that there are risks in becoming so preoccupied with processes as to lose sight of objectives; that as strategy needs to be informed by policy, so policy needs to be informed by a clear vision of the national interest, framed with a keen sensitivity to both ideals and capabilities. Our position in the world, Kennan has repeatedly argued, depends largely on what we ourselves make it:

> If we wish our relations with Russia to be normal and serene, the best thing we can do is to see that on our side, at least, they are given the outward aspect of normalcy and serenity. Form means a great deal in international life. . . . What is important, in other words, is not so much *what* is done as *how* it is done. And in this sense, good form in outward demeanor becomes more than a means to an end, more than a subsidiary attribute: it becomes a value in itself, with its own validity and its own effectiveness, and perhaps— human nature being what it is—the greatest value of all.[30]

In an age when security is acknowledged to be a relative and not an absolute concept, hinging not so much on what configuration of power actually exists as on how it is perceived, it is well to be reminded that we have the ability to shape those perceptions to a considerable extent through the manner in which we bear ourselves. Self-confidence, by this logic, becomes more than just good psychology; it is nothing less than a key determinant of power in the world today.

Michael Howard has written of Clausewitz that he "had less cause to fear his critics than to be wary of many of his professed admirers."[31] The same might be said of Kennan as well, for like the Prussian strategist's great work *On War*, the "X" article was put to uses its author could hardly have foreseen. It was no accident that Kennan came to harbor a certain lack of confidence "in the ability of men to define hypothetically in any useful way . . . future situations which no one could really imagine or envisage."[32]

And yet, there is in Kennan's writings a degree of foresight and a consistency of strategic vision for which it would be difficult to find a contemporary parallel. Kennan is not often regarded as a strategist, but if "strategy" is thought of as the rational relationship of national objectives to national capabilities, then he has as good a claim as anyone to having devised a coherent American strategy for dealing with the postwar world.

The concerns which produced that strategy probably will not dominate events of the next decade to the extent that they have the past three. Dilemmas of economics, ecology, race and technology all are likely to overshadow in importance traditional sources of Soviet-American antagonism; these issues tend to cut across old cold war fault lines. The test of lasting relevance, however, is the extent to which principles developed in one context can be fruitfully applied in others. If the continued pertinence of the ideas Kennan worked out during the early years of the cold war is any guide, his strategic concepts, like those of Clausewitz, may find application in circumstances far removed from those which gave rise to them. One can only hope that the full range of Kennan's writings will be taken as text, though, and not just the misleading, but eminently persuasive, "X" article.

NOTES

[1]George F. Kennan, *Memoirs: 1925-1950,* Boston: Little Brown, 1967, p. 356.

[2]See, for example, Eduard M. Mark, "What Kind of Containment?" in Thomas G. Paterson, ed., *Containment and the Cold War,* Reading, Mass.: Addison-Wesley, 1973, pp. 96-109; and C. Ben Wright, "Mr. 'X' and Containment," *Slavic Review,* XXXV, March 1976, pp. 1-31.

[3]Walter Lippmann, *The Cold War: A Study in U.S. Foreign Policy,* New York: Harper, 1947. See also Charles Gati, "What Containment Meant," *Foreign Policy,* No. 7, Summer 1972, pp. 24-36; and Thomas G. Paterson, "The Search for Meaning: George F. Kennan and American Foreign Policy," in Frank J. Merli and Theodore A. Wilson, eds., *Makers of American Foreign Policy,* New York: Scribner, 1974, pp. 575-576.

[4]Joseph M. Jones, *The Fifteen Weeks (February 21-June 5, 1947),* New York: Viking, 1955, pp. 154-155; Kennan to Dean Acheson, May 23, 1947, *Foreign Relations of the United States: 1947 (hereinafter Foreign Relations: 1947),* III, Washington: GPO, p. 229; Kennan National War College lecture, "Planning of Foreign Policy," June 18, 1947, George F. Kennan Papers (hereinafter Kennan Papers), Princeton University, Box 17; PPS 4, "Certain Aspects of the European Recovery Program from the United States Standpoint (Preliminary Report)," July 23, 1947, Policy Planning Files, Department of State.

[5]PPS 13, "Resumé of World Situation," November 6, 1947, *Foreign Relations: 1947,* I, pp. 772-773.

[6]PPS 23, "Review of Current Trends: U.S. Foreign Policy," February 24, 1948, *Foreign Relations: 1948,* I, pp. 524-525; Kennan to George C. Marshall, March 14, 1948, *ibid.,* p. 534. See also Kennan's presentation to the Secretary of the Navy's Council, January 14, 1948, Kennan Papers, Box 17.

[7]Kennan, *Memoirs: 1925-1950,* p. 359.

[8]See, for example, Kennan's National War College lecture, "Contemporary Problems of Foreign Policy," September 17, 1948, Kennan Papers, Box 17.

[9]Unpublished Kennan paper, "The Soviet Way of Thought and Its Effect on Foreign Policy," January 24, 1947, Kennan Papers, Box 16.

[10]Lippmann, *The Cold War,* pp. 31, 33-34, 40.

[11]Kennan, *loc. cit.,* Footnote 9.

[12]Kennan University of Virginia lecture, "Russian-American Relations," February 20, 1947, Kennan Papers, Box 16.

[13]PPS 23, February 24, 1948, *Foreign Relations: 1948,* I, p. 519. See also Kennan notes for Secretary of State Marshall, July 21, 1947, *Foreign Relations: 1947,* III, p. 335.

[14]PPS 35, "The Attitude of This Government Towards Events in Yugoslavia," June 30, 1948, *Foreign Relations: 1948,* IV, p. 1081; NSC 58/2, "United States Policy Toward the Soviet Satellite States in Eastern Europe," December 8, 1949, National Security Council Files, Modern Military Records Division, National Archives, GPO. See also PPS 39/1, "U.S. Policy Toward China," November 23, 1948, *Foreign Relations: 1948,* VIII, p. 208.

[15]PPS 38, "United States Objectives With Respect to Russia," August 18, 1948, Policy Planning Staff Files, Department of State.

[16]Kennan talk to the Board of Governors of the Federal Reserve System, December 1, 1947, and to the Secretary of the Navy's Council, December 3, 1947, Kennan Papers, Box 17. See also George F. Kennan, *Realities of American Foreign Policy,* Princeton: Princeton University Press, 1954, p. 76.

[17]Lippmann, *The Cold War,* pp. 35, 59.

[18]Transcript, Kennan post-lecture comment, National War College, September 16, 1946, Kennan Papers, Box 16. See also Kennan National War College lecture, "Soviet Diplomacy," October 6, 1947, *ibid.*, Box 17; Kennan talk to Business Advisory Committee, Department of Commerce, September 24, 1947, *ibid.;* and PPS 13, November 6, 1947, *Foreign Relations: 1947*, I, p. 772.

[19]PPS 23, February 24, 1948, No. I, p. 522; Kennan to Lippmann, April 6, 1948, Kennan Papers, Box 17.

[20]PPS 38, August 18, 1948.

[21]Kennan, *Memoirs: 1925-1950*, pp. 363-367.

[22]*Ibid.*, p. 365; interview with George F. Kennan, Princeton, New Jersey, February 2, 1977.

[23]PPS 43, "Considerations Affecting the Conclusion of a North Atlantic Security Pact," November 24, 1948, *Foreign Relations: 1948*, III, p. 286.

[24]Kennan, *Memoirs: 1925-1950*, pp. 316-319, 484-486. See also PPS 13, November 6, 1947, *Foreign Relations: 1947*, p. 776.

[25]See Kennan, *Memoirs: 1925-1950*, p. 497; and George F. Kennan, "The United States and the Soviet Union, 1917-1976," *Foreign Affairs,* July 1976, pp. 681-682.

[26]NSC 68, "United States Objectives and Programs for National Security," April 14, 1950, *Naval War College Review*, Vol. XXVII, No. 6, May-June 1975, pp. 51-108. See also Paul Y. Hammond, "NSC 68: Prologue to Rearmament," in Warner Schilling, Paul Y. Hammond, and Glenn H. Snyder, eds., *Strategy, Politics, and Defense Budgets*, New York: Columbia University Press, 1962, pp. 267-278.

[27]It is interesting to note in this connection that Kennan, in May 1948, recommended that the CIA be given a covert political action capability, with the understanding that its employment would be strictly controlled by the Departments of State, Defense, and the National Security Council. "It did not work out at all the way I had conceived it," he later admitted. Quoted in Anne Karalekas, "History of the Central Intelligence Agency," in U.S. Senate, 94th Cong., 2nd Sess., Select Committee to Study Government Operations With Respect to Intelligence Activities, *Final Report: Supplementary Detailed Staff Reports on Foreign and Military Intelligence: Book IV*, Washington: GPO, 1976, p. 31. See also George F. Kennan, *Memoirs: 1950-1963*, Boston: Little Brown, 1972, pp. 202-203.

[28]Kennan, *Memoirs: 1925-1950*, p. 130.

[29]Kennan to Marshall and Robert Lovett, August 5, 1948, *Foreign Relations: 1948*, I, p. 599.

[30]Kennan, University of Virginia lecture, February 20, 1947, Kennan Papers, Box 16.

[31]Michael Howard, "The Influence of Clausewitz," in Carl von Clausewitz, *On War*, ed. and trans. by Michael Howard and Peter Paret, Princeton: Princeton University Press, 1976, p. 28.

[32]Kennan, *Memoirs: 1925-1950*, p. 408.

12. Mr. "X" Is Inconsistent and Wrong

Eduard Mark

A young scholar, Eduard Mark recently completed a dissertation on the interpretation of Soviet foreign policy in the United States between 1928 and 1947, at the University of Connecticut. The present essay was written in response to the one by Professor Gaddis (selection 11). Mark accuses Gaddis of selective quotations to prove his point. Drawing on the same body of public and private sources and with documentation from Kennan's own words, Mark says the evidence clearly demonstrates that Kennan advocated—after the publication of his "X" article—a far more vigorous and comprehensive concept of containment than he or Gaddis now admits. In many places Kennan, says Mark, insisted that U.S. military power actively deployed was essential to the containment of Soviet ambition and power—and not only with respect to the most highly industrialized non-Communist countries.

IN THE JULY 1977 ISSUE OF FOREIGN AFFAIRS, which marked the thirtieth anniversary of the appearance in its pages of George F. Kennan's famous "X" article, "The Sources of Soviet Conduct," John Lewis Gaddis ambitiously attempted to resolve once and for all the seemingly interminable controversy that has surrounded Kennan's call for containment ever since that first public enunciation. Diplomatic historians doubtless noted with interest that Professor Gaddis contends, quite categorically, that the retrospective elucidation of containment found in the first volume of Kennan's *Memoirs* is wholly satisfactory with respect to what have been far and away its most controversial features: to wit, the assertions that the policy was "political" rather than "military," and that it was to be cautiously implemented within strictly defined geographical limits rather narrower than had commonly been supposed.

The burden of this essay is that Kennan's belated apologia was misleading, and that Gaddis errs in his reconstruction of containment as regards the crucial questions of its means and scope. For neither in life itself nor in Kennan's postwar writings can "political" and "military" measures be so sharply distinguished as the onetime policymaker's reminiscences suggest. And, while containment was certainly no rationale for uninhibited global intervention, fundamental objectives and concerns of the policy tended to promote a broader interventionism than Kennan admits or Gaddis realizes.[1]

Professor Gaddis bases his reconstruction of containment in some measure on Kennan's denial that communist ideology was a "determinant of Soviet policy." While probably not without some effect on the Soviet leadership's perceptions of political realities, communism was essentially a façade: domestically it provided a legitimizing myth for a usurping regime; in the realm of foreign affairs it cloaked Russian "national interests" with the appearance of beneficent purpose and made willing stooges of gullible foreign revolutionaries. Disposing of ideology as a "determinant," however, raises an obvious question that Gaddis does not really answer: How then did Kennan account for Soviet expansionism? He states only that the diplomat believed that the Soviet leaders felt toward the West a deep hostility that sprang from a sense of "insecurity," itself the product of Russia's unhappy past and their own conspiratorial backgrounds. Presumably, therefore, the object of Soviet expansionism was security.

This rendering of Kennan's portrayal of Soviet motives is not so much incorrect as it is incomplete—so incomplete that the flavor of Kennan's warnings about Soviet expansionism is lost along with some of the dimensions of containment. If, for example, a desire for national security explained Russian actions, one might reasonably conclude that a tier of buffer states constituted the limit of the U.S.S.R.'s hegemonic aspirations. But the apostle of containment was most explicit that the Soviet objective was "world revolution," "the destruction of capitalism everywhere," and that the United States itself was menaced by "a great political force" intent upon its "destruction."[2]

Had he taken his own advice and delved deeper into the documents he produces as a *deus ex machina* to redeem Kennan's *Memoirs* and to prove that the "X" article was not a "definitive statement of containment" (as though any historian of the last 20 years or so had attempted to analyze the policy without recourse to other documents), Gaddis would have seen that, in Kennan's estimation, the "insecurity" that afflicted Stalin and his henchmen was of a very special type. It was the product not only—indeed not so much—of Russian history and the personal backgrounds of its leaders as of the dictatorial form of government they had imposed on a long-suffering people. This latter anxiety had a very dire consequence for other nations: because of it Soviet totalitarianism was the functional equivalent, the analogue, of classical world revolutionary Marxism-Leninism, quite without regard to whether Stalin took that doctrine seriously or not.

Until early 1946, Kennan explained Soviet expansionism much as Gaddis states that he did: he traced it to Russia's traditional sense of vulnerability, exacerbated by Marxist suspicions, although thinking it "questionable" that ideology animated "to any appreciable degree the power of the Kremlin."[3] Insofar as domestic imperatives bore upon Soviet aggressiveness, it was probably in that Stalin's heavy reliance on the specter of "capitalist encirclement" to justify his dictatorship precluded any reliance upon collective security arrangements such as the United Nations, lest there be created the appearance of a community of interest between the Soviet Union and the bourgeois states.[4]

But with his famous "Long Telegram" of February 22, 1946, Kennan began to argue that Soviet totalitarianism imbued Soviet expansionism with potentially unlimited ambitions. He wrote that the Soviet hierarchy sensed that its rule was "relatively fragile in its psychological foundations, unable to withstand comparison or contact with political systems of Western countries." The Soviet Union, therefore, sought "security only in patient but deadly struggle for the total destruction of rival power, never in compacts or compromises with it."[5] In the unsent letter to Walter Lippmann cited by Gaddis, Kennan stated explicitly that Soviet tyranny was threatened by the existence of freedom anywhere:

> It is the Russians, not we, who cannot afford a world half slave and half free. The contrasts implicit in such a world are intolerable to the fictions on which their power rests. *The final establishment of communist principles can only be universal.* It assumes a Stygian darkness. If one ray of light of individual dignity or inquiry is permitted, the effort must ultimately fail.[6]

In short, while the security of *Russia as a state* could be assured by a limited sphere of influence, the security of the *Soviet totalitarian system* required the subjugation of as much of the world as possible to dictatorial controls approximating those in the Soviet Union.

On March 15, 1948, Kennan warned Secretary of State George C. Marshall that a Russian invasion of Western Europe might be imminent. While he had previously supposed that the Soviets would avoid a "military contest" with the United States, the recent coup in Czechoslovakia had led him to revise that estimate. It now appeared that they might resort to outright conquest, at once lured by the prospect of an easy victory and driven by the fear that there could be no final consolidation of their position in Eastern Europe as long as there remained an independent "Western civilization" to act as an economic and political lodestone for the peoples of that region—a clear application of his thesis that ultimately the maintenance of totalitarian control required the elimination of all that furnished a basis for invidious comparison.[7]

Ordinarily, Kennan bade his countrymen "distinguish what is indeed progressive social doctrine from the rivalry of a foreign political machine which has appropriated and abused the slogans of socialism."[8] Occasionally, however, he spoke of Soviet expansionism as though it were ideologically motivated because it was rhetorically effective to do so and because his analysis amounted to the same thing in a practical sense. Thus he warned one audience that the Soviet objective was "world revolution," but added that this early Bolshevik objective had been retained because "for reasons too intricate to go into here, it has become closely associated with internal political conditions in the Soviet Union; and the men in the Kremlin could not depart from it, even if they wished to."[9] (The "X" article is to a degree an example of

Kennan's resorting to ideological rhetoric.[10]) Gaddis has, in short, small warrant for distinguishing Kennan from those who used communist ideology as a "predictive instrument" and thus presented the "Soviet threat in global terms."

Military vs. Political Containment

It is safe to say that nothing in Kennan's *Memoirs* has inspired more skepticism than the disclaimer that he had envisioned "not the containment by military means of a military threat, but the political containment of a political threat."[11] "Political" and "military" are not often—*pace* Clausewitz—opposed in such fashion with respect to international relations, and one must suppose that Kennan thought that the Soviet threat was of an unusually pacific nature for this blunt juxtaposition to be warranted. Professor Gaddis certainly does. He writes that Kennan believed fears of a Soviet attack "groundless," and then blithely quotes a highly equivocal statement the diplomat made in October 1947 to the effect that ". . . as things stand today, it is not Russian military power which is threatening us, it is Russian political power. . . . If it is not entirely a military threat, I doubt it can be effectively met entirely by military means. . . ."

In point of fact, the assertion that Kennan believed that the Soviet threat was solely "political" in a sense opposed to "military" flies in the face of much documentary evidence. And the statement that containment was "political" in a similar sense presupposes, as we shall see, a very special definition of that word. Kennan was a consistent advocate of "a powerful and impressive military establishment, commensurate with the responsibilities we are forced to bear in the life of the world community."[12] Statesmen, to be sure, value military strength as a matter of course. But Kennan's advocacy also proceeded from a very specific postulate: that overt aggression by the armed forces of the Soviet Union was possible in certain circumstances. (In the October 1947 statement quoted by Gaddis the emphasis should be placed on "today.")

In the late summer of 1946, President Truman's Special Counsel, Clark M. Clifford, and his assistant, George M. Elsey, prepared at the Chief Executive's request an evaluation of the cold war entitled "American Relations with the Soviet Union." Since its publication in the memoirs of the late Arthur Krock, this document has been contrasted by Gaddis and others with Kennan's "political" containment because of its conclusion that "the main deterrent to Soviet attack on our territory, or on areas vital to our security, will be the military power of this country."[13]

When the first draft of "American Relations with the Soviet Union" was completed in September 1946, a copy was sent to Kennan for his comments. "I think the tone is excellent," he replied, "and I have no fault to find with it." He endorsed with particular emphasis the report's call for the development of nuclear and biological weapons, adding that it was "important this country be *prepared* to use them if need be, for the mere fact of such preparedness may prove to be the only deterrent to Russian aggressive actions and in this sense the only sure guarantee of peace." (At his suggestions these words were included in the final draft.[14]) Kennan also warned that when the Soviets developed atomic weapons they "would not hesitate for a moment to apply this power against us if by so doing they thought they might materially improve their own power position in the world."[15]

Kennan thought war unlikely not because of the intrinsically "political" character of Soviet expansionism, but because the Soviets were "still weaker by far than the capitalist world" and understood that "if they were to become involved with a superior force, it might lead to catastrophe for them."[16] His assurance on this score was far from complete, however, as the March 1948 warning to Secretary of State Marshall unmistakably shows. Moreover, while American military strength might deter overt Soviet aggression, it also redirected Soviet expansionism into other channels. Kennan warned that insofar as the U.S.S.R. was deterred from open aggression, it would seek to realize its hegemonic designs covertly through the subversive manipulation of foreign communist parties and allied and duped groups of every description. He often epitomized Soviet policy by stating that it sought "a maximum of power with a minimum of responsibility," and from this expectation derived the second, *active* use he foresaw for military power: its role in containing indirect Soviet aggression.[17]

In his *Memoirs* Kennan provides a definition of the "political" threat he perceived. First in his columns and then in his book *The Cold War*, Walter Lippmann assumed that the newly famous Mr. "X" was predicting a series of invasions by the Red Army. To explain his actual fears Kennan refers to a letter he wrote (but did not actually send) to the journalist in April 1948:

The Russians don't want to invade anyone. It is not in their tradition. They tried it once in Finland and got their fingers burned. Above all, they don't want the open responsibility that official invasion brings with it. They far prefer to do the job politically with stooge forces. Note well: when I say politically that does not mean without violence. But it means that the violence is nominally *domestic*, not *international* violence.[18]

The difficulty with this passage (apart from reconciling it with the solemn warning to Marshall of not two months before) lies in the arbitrary use of "political" to describe Soviet-inspired civil or guerrilla wars. Even if this be allowed on the questionable grounds that the violence in question was "nominally domestic," it by no means follows that containment was to be exclusively "political" in any sense consonant with ordinary usage. While Kennan was of the opinion that "the use of U.S. regular forces to oppose the efforts of indigenous communist elements must generally be considered as a risky and profitless undertaking," he did not categorically rule out such intervention.[19]

In 1946, aware of the "imperative need for acceptance of limited warfare," Kennan began to urge the creation of "small, compact, alert forces, capable of delivering at short notice effective blows in limited theaters of operation far from our own shores."[20] Succeeding years showed the uses he envisioned for the "alert forces." In December 1947 (if we may trust a rapporteur's notes) he contemplated the use of American forces in Greece.[21] Four months later, in any event, he unequivocally advocated military intervention in Italy. Greatly worried by the prospect of a communist victory in the forthcoming elections, Kennan proposed that the ostensibly independent Italian government "outlaw" the Communist Party. The civil war sure to result would give the United States

> grounds for the reoccupation of the Foggia fields or any other facilities we might wish. This would admittedly result in much violence and probably a military division of Italy; but we are getting close to the deadline and I think it might well be preferable to a bloodless election victory, unopposed by ourselves, which would give the Communists the entire peninsula at one coup and send waves of panic to all surrounding areas.[22]

Kennan also urged intervention in Korea, and regarded American unpreparedness for that conflict as proof of the need for "alert forces."[23] In a magazine article of 1951, moreover, he directly linked Korea with containment, writing that the "X" article of four years before had foreseen just such attacks as that on South Korea. This is a claim that may well be believed, for as Kennan had warned in the 1940s that the Soviets would seek "maximum power" with "minimum responsibility" through the use of "stooge forces," so his contemporary judgment on the Korean War was that, seeing an opportunity for expansion "at relatively little risk to themselves," they had unleashed their "Korean puppets."[24]

There was undeniably a "political" aspect to containment. Kennan was an author of the Marshall Plan and incontestably believed that improved socioeconomic conditions were of the greatest importance in fostering resistance to Soviet expansionism.[25] But as he himself wrote, "The fiber of political resistance among our allies to Moscow Communist pressure will be deeply affected by the extent to which they continue to feel themselves secure in the military sense."[26] "Political" measures alone, however, would neither deter Soviet invasion nor quell armed subversion. Indeed, given the peculiar susceptibilities of Soviet totalitarianism, successful "political" containment might, insofar as it created viable democracies, even prompt Soviet aggression in one form or another. (Kennan's March 1948 warning to Marshall should be recalled in this regard.) It was necessary, therefore, to contain the Soviets *"both militarily and politically."*[27]

The Breadth of Containment

Arguments about the scope of containment admit of less precision than those about the means since they concern questions of degree rather than of kind. It may be said, however, that Gaddis takes in a rather literal way the impression Kennan seeks to give in his *Memoirs* that containment, as originally conceived, was precisely circumscribed in a geographical sense. Gaddis adduces several arguments in favor of a "narrow" containment, none of which is compelling. Correctly observing that Kennan distinguished between communism and Soviet expansionism, Gaddis assumes that containment had a limited purview because it was directed at the latter and not necessarily at radical movements drawing their inspiration from the former. This conclusion, however, does not follow because, as we have seen, Kennan deemed the ambitions of Soviet expansionism essentially unlimited and argued that they would work through the many radical movements around the world whose allegiance the Soviet Union commanded. In opposing that expansionism, therefore, American policy would at times inevitably have to oppose radical movements, however tolerant of left-wing ideology it might be in principle.

Professor Gaddis also notes that Kennan appreciated that American resources were finite and that he doubted the need for containment "beyond the reach of Soviet military or police power" because he thought it unlikely that a communist regime could long survive without direct Russian support or that if one did it would willingly remain a tool of Soviet imperialism.

The first of these arguments really tells us little since any policy must be limited necessarily by the means available to implement it, and it is not shown that Kennan believed American resources to be more limited than did other policymakers.[28] The second argument overlooks the simple facts that the Soviet Union is by far the largest nation in the world, sprawling as it does over Europe and Asia, and that clearly a great deal of territory falls within its "reach"—even when one exempts East and Southeast Asia (including China) from the purview of containment, as Kennan did in 1948.[29] His alarmed reaction to the prospect of an electoral victory by the Italian Communists, even then the most independent in Western Europe (thanks to the intellectual legacy of Antonio Gramsci and the leadership of Palmiro Togliatti), suggests that in practice Kennan was not prepared to gamble on either the viability or the autonomy of communist governments. It is arguable that before Tito's final June 1948 break with Moscow, Italy could be regarded as within "the reach of Soviet military or police power." But in that case the Italian episode must be regarded as an example of how much territory that reach encompassed.

At first reading the most convincing of Gaddis' arguments for a "limited" containment is the undeniable fact that in 1948 Kennan argued that the principal task before American foreign policy was to preserve from Soviet control the as yet non-communist major industrial regions: Great Britain, the Rhine Valley, and Japan. A moment's reflection, however, will suggest that it by no means follows that a policy designed to protect those regions was necessarily to be implemented in or even near them. (Gaddis assumes that it does, and describes containment as "a limited application of effort in a few key locations.") The most obvious objection to such an inference is that modern industrial societies (particularly those of the three regions mentioned) are highly dependent upon the natural resources of the underdeveloped world. We have, of course, had this fact rudely called to our attention in recent years, but it was no less appreciated during and after the Second World War, as evidenced by Allied relations in Iran, the Anglo-American rivalry in Saudi Arabia or State Department opposition to the recognition of Israel. (Kennan himself referred to the dependence of Western Europe on Middle Eastern oil in the document Gaddis cites to support his point about Kennan's emphasis on the industrial areas.[30])

Even disregarding the obvious facts of economic dependence, containment could be restricted to the major industrial regions only if at least one of two propositions were true: that Kennan believed Soviet expansionism would be directed only against those areas and/or that he thought the United States might with impunity ignore Soviet thrusts elsewhere. But both are demonstrably false. In 1946 he warned that the Soviets would seek to weaken Western influence in colonial and backward areas in the belief that ''insofar as the policy is successful there will be created a vacuum which will favor communist-Soviet penetration.'' Later the same year he wrote that the Russians planned to make Turkey ''a puppet state, which will serve as a springboard for the domination of the eastern Mediterranean.''[31] Kennan plainly thought these challenges could not be ignored. In 1947, for example, he limited containment to ''highly strategic areas'' where the victory of communism would have serious consequences for the United States, but spoke of backward Greece in the same breath as Germany.[32]

There were several reasons why Kennan's concept of strategic importance embraced underdeveloped countries. He greatly feared, first of all, the moral consequences of communist victories. He supported the Truman Doctrine on the grounds that the fall of Greece and Turkey would facilitate Soviet penetration of the Middle East. Soviet gains there, he argued, might propel the communist parties of Western Europe into power and drive England into neutrality.[33] As we have seen, in 1948 he advocated intervention in Italy with the argument that a communist electoral victory would produce panic in the surrounding areas. His reasons for supporting the intervention in Korea were similar.[34] Gaddis is not unaware of this psychological ''domino theory'' but describes it as an ''unanticipated difficulty'' that arose from the need to calm the fears of those peoples in whom containment sought to instill a sense of self-confidence. His failure to understand that it was an intrinsic part of Kennan's conception of strategic importance (which was never narrowly geographical), coeval with containment itself, is surprising because he correctly stresses "the extent to which Kennan's strategy relied upon psychology."

It is also interesting to note that there are indications that during 1949 and 1950 Kennan moved away from his emphasis of 1948 on the importance of the major industrialized regions toward a less discriminating conception of geographical importance. In 1948 he viewed the prospect of a communist victory in China with relative equanimity, but in August 1949 he described the impending triumph of Mao Tse-tung as "a catastrophe not only for the people of China but for the prospects for stability and peace throughout the Far East."[35] The following November he described at some length the conditions under which the United States should extend aid to nations imperiled by Soviet expansionism without mentioning any test of strategic importance.[36] And in February 1950 he warned that if the Soviets succeeded

> by means short of war, in bringing under their influence the remaining non-Communist countries of Europe and Asia, our security would be more subtly (but perhaps as dangerously) undermined than by an atomic attack on our territory. For the world balance of power would then be turned, at least temporarily, against us.

Therefore, Kennan concluded, the United States "must continue the policy of throwing its weight into the balance *wherever there are relatively good chances* that it will be effective in preventing the further spread of the power of international communism."[37]

Furthermore, one of the fundamental purposes of containment militated against basing the policy upon a purely geopolitical foundation. Kennan maintained that the "possibilities for American policy are by no means limited to holding the line and hoping for the best. It is entirely possible for the United States to influence by its actions the internal developments, both within Russia and throughout the international Communist movement, by which Russian policy is largely determined." Indeed, the United States had it

> in its power to increase enormously the strains under which Soviet policy must operate . . . and in this way to promote tendencies which must eventually find their outlet in either the breakup or the gradual mellowing of Soviet power. For no mystical, Messianic movement—and particularly not that of the Kremlin—can face frustration indefinitely without eventually adjusting itself in one way or another to the logic of that state of affairs.[38]

In part, the mellowing or destruction of Soviet power was to be encompassed by demonstrating the viability of the American way of life, by giving the lie to the "keystone of Communist philosophy," the belief in the "palsied decrepitude of the capitalist world."[39] But it was also to be accomplished by frustrating Soviet expansionism—which Kennan likened to a "fluid stream which moves wherever it is permitted to move"—"indefinitely."[40] He argued in 1947 that

> if you could start rolling back the international Communist movement today, if you could bring about a set of circumstances where they are not making the first downs but where somebody else was making the first downs time after time against them, I think you might see a general crumbling of Russian influence and prestige which would carry beyond . . . the satellite countries, and into the heart of the Soviet Union itself. Now, that is why I feel what we are trying to do in the case of Greece and Turkey is of such vital importance, because if it is successful, it is going to have that type of effect.[41]

This aspect of containment, it will be observed, is mentioned neither in Kennan's *Memoirs* nor in Gaddis' article. The reasons for the omission in the one and the oversight in the other are, it may be presumed, one and the same: insofar as containment was intended as an indirect assault on the Soviet system through the constant frustration of the Soviet drive for universal dominion it had a purpose that transcended the importance of specific areas. It could not consequently be limited to those areas.

It is in fact highly probable that Kennan's indignant insistence that containment was not open-ended stems not so much from limits inherent in the policy itself as from the faith he once had in the capacity of containment to exacerbate certain fundamental weaknesses in the Soviet system. These were, as Gaddis notes, serious. They included the problem of succession after Stalin's death, a demoralized population, pervasive economic incompetence, and the problems of holding in submission the more civilized peoples of Eastern Europe. At one point in 1945 Kennan permitted himself to believe that "another five or ten years should find Russia overshadowed by those clouds of civil disintegration that darkened the Russian sky at the outset of the century."[42] In his unsent letter of 1948 to Lippmann he was at pains to refute the argument that "containment was a passive, negative policy which, even if successful, would solve nothing and would oblige us to remain indefinitely, armed to the teeth, trying to defend a long series of over-extended positions. . . ." He mentioned, however, *not one* of the limitations he had previously discussed in connection with the policy, rather writing that he was tried by the assertion that containment meant indefinite and indeterminate confrontation,

> because I thought I had pointed out, in the X article, that the Russians, too, are made of flesh and blood; that time has a habit of running out on them, just as it does on other people; and that we had good reason to hope that some of the internal contradictions of their own system would eventually catch up with them. . . .

It was not necessary, Kennan continued, "to draw up any program for the defeat of Soviet power, if we can only be successful in the policies we are now pursuing. The Russians will defeat themselves."[43]

Containment, in summary, was partially "political" in that Kennan understood that pervasive socioeconomic discontent was fertile soil for communist subversion. But it was also military in that he believed that the polymorphous impulses of Soviet expansionism could, as it were, be channeled into "containable" subversion only as long as the superior power of the United States assured the failure of overt aggression. It was equally so because Kennan expected the local minions of Soviet expansionism to resort, as in Greece and Korea, to the "nominally domestic" violence of insurrection and civil war and thus advocated armed intervention where indigenous resistance was unequal to the task.

Kennan was also of the opinion that the boundless ambitions of Soviet totalitarianism would be responsible for, or at least seek to take advantage of, a goodly portion of the world's revolutionary ferment. This expectation, together with his concern for the world balance of power, his fear of the psychological consequences of Soviet successes, and his belief that the constant frustration of Soviet expansionism would promote desirable changes in the U.S.S.R., tended in practice to erode his reservations about a policy of broad purview.

NOTES

[1]John Lewis Gaddis, "Containment: A Reassessment," *Foreign Affairs* July 1977, pp. 873-887. Kennan's explanation of containment may be found in his *Memoirs: 1925-1950*, Boston: Little, Brown, 1967, pp. 354-367.

[2]George F. Kennan, "Current Problems of Soviet-American Relations," May 9, 1947, George F. Kennan Papers (hereinafter cited Kennan Papers) at the Princeton University Library, Princeton, New Jersey. See also Kennan, *op. cit.*, p. 351.

[3]*Ibid.*, "Russia—Seven Years Later," pp. 519-520; *ibid.*, "Russia's International Position at the Close of the War with Germany," p. 537. In the same volume, see "Telegraphic Message from Moscow of February 22, 1946," p. 533.

[4]See, for example, *ibid.*, "Russia—Seven Years Later," pp. 517-518 and Kennan to James F. Byrnes, October 4, 1946, *Foreign Relations of the United States, 1945* (hereinafter cited *FRUS/1945*), V, Washington: GPO, 1967, pp. 888-891.

[5]Kennan, *op. cit.*, "Telegraphic Message of February 22, 1946," p. 550. Kennan stated that Czarist absolutism had been subject to the same compulsion—a token of his essentially unideological analysis.

[6]Unsent letter to Walter Lippmann (emphasis added), April 6, 1948, Kennan Papers. This argument is strongly stated in another document found in Kennan's Papers, "Foreign Aid in the Framework of National Policy," November 10, 1949. See also George F. Kennan, "America and the Russian Future," *Foreign Affairs*, April 1951, p. 114. One observer noted that in conversation Kennan "talks sparingly of democracy and communism. . . . He bases his thinking on the 'profound differences between the liberal and the totalitarian concepts of human society'. . . ." Brooks Atkinson, "America's Global Planner," *New York Times Magazine*, July 13, 1947, p. 9.

[7]Kennan to George C. Marshall, March 15, 1948, *FRUS/1948*, III, Washington: GPO, 1974, pp. 848-849. It will be instructive to compare this cable with Kennan, *Memoirs: 1925-1950*, p. 400.

[8]*Ibid.*, p. 301.

[9]"Current Problems," *supra*, footnote 2.

[10]See, for example, George F. Kennan ("X"), "The Sources of Soviet Conduct," *Foreign Affairs*, July 1947, p. 574 and p. 582. The "X" article also stresses the implications of the Soviet political system for the U.S.S.R.'s external relations at pp. 569-571. Upon close examination, all of Kennan's references to Soviet "dogma" stress its role as a "figleaf" for motives quite unrelated to world revolution. The emphasis placed upon ideology in so much writing about Kennan—and the early cold war generally—is the product of hindsight, affected by later events.

[11]Kennan, *Memoirs: 1925-1950*, p. 358.

[12]George F. Kennan, "The International Situation," *The Department of State Bulletin*, XXI, September 5, 1949, p. 324. Kennan said on one occasion, ". . . I think we should follow the classic advice of Theodore Roosevelt: to speak softly and carry a big stick," "Current Problems," *supra*, footnote 2.

[13]"American Relations with the Soviet Union," in Arthur C. Krock, *Memoirs: Sixty Years on the Firing Line*, New York: Funk and Wagnalls, 1948, p. 477. See also John Lewis Gaddis, *The United States and the Origins of the Cold War*, New York: Columbia University Press, 1972, pp. 322-323.

[14]Kennan to Clark M. Clifford (Kennan's emphasis), September 16, 1946, George M. Elsey Papers at the Harry S. Truman Library, Independence, Missouri, Box 63. This memorandum is not signed by Kennan but is identified as his by a marginal notation in Elsey's handwriting. Mr. Clifford and Mr. Elsey have kindly confirmed Kennan's au-

thorship; Clifford to the author, June 10, 1975, enclosing Elsey to Clark M. Clifford, June 3, 1975. Compare this sentence with Krock, *op. cit.*, p. 478.

[15]Kennan to James F. Byrnes, September 30, 1945, *FRUS/1945*, V, pp. 884-886.

[16]Kennan to Clark M. Clifford, *op. cit.* See also "Telegraphic Message of February 22, 1946," *supra,* footnote 3, p. 558; Kennan, *supra*, footnote 10, p. 281.

[17]For a list of prospective Soviet agents, see *op. cit.*, "Telegraphic Message of February 22, 1946," pp. 554-555. For this characteristic of Soviet policy see "Russia's National Objectives," April 10, 1947, Kennan Papers; Kennan to James F. Byrnes, July 15, 1945, *FRUS/1945*, V, pp. 866-868; and Kennan to Carmel Offie, May 10, 1946, *FRUS/1946*, V, Washington: GPO, 1969, pp. 555-556.

[18]Kennan, *Memoirs: 1925-1950*, p. 361 (Kennan's emphasis), and pp. 219-220.

[19]*Ibid.*, p. 380.

[20]*Ibid.* See also Kennan's address to the National Defense Committee of the Chamber of Commerce of the United States, January 23, 1947, Kennan Papers.

[21]Memorandum of conversation by John D. Jernegan, December 26, 1947, *FRUS/1947*, V, Washington: GPO, 1971, pp. 466-469.

[22]Kennan to George C. Marshall, March 15, 1948, *FRUS/1948*, III, pp. 848-849.

[23]Kennan, *Memoirs: 1925-1950*, p. 312.

[24]George F. Kennan, "Let Peace Not Die of Neglect," *The New York Times Magazine*, February 25, 1951, p. 41.

[25]See, for example, Kennan to George C. Marshall, May 23, 1947, enclosing "Policy with Respect to American Aid to Western Europe: Views of the Policy Planning Staff," *FRUS/1947*, III, Washington: GPO, 1972, pp. 223-230; Kennan, *supra*, footnote 10, pp. 581-582; "Telegraphic Message of February 22, 1946," *supra,* footnote 3, p. 559, and "Current Problems," *supra,* footnote 2.

[26]George F. Kennan, "Is War with Russia Inevitable?," *The Department of State Bulletin*, XXII, February 20, 1950, p. 271.

[27]George F. Kennan transcript of lecture to State Department personnel, September 17, 1946, Kennan Papers (emphasis added).

[28]Gaddis notes, for example, that Kennan thought it beyond this country's ability to deal with China effectively. But this was also the dominant belief in the Truman Administration. See, for example, Dean Acheson, *Present at the Creation: My Years in the State Department*, New York: Signet Books, 1970, pp. 463-465 and pp. 400-403.

[29]George F. Kennan, "Contemporary Problems of Foreign Policy," September 17, 1948, Kennan Papers.

[30]*Ibid.*

[31]"Telegraphic Message of February 22, 1946," *supra,* footnote 3, p. 553 and p. 555; Kennan to Clark M. Clifford, September 6, 1946, Elsey Papers.

[32]George F. Kennan, "Problems of U.S. Foreign Policy after Moscow," May 6, 1947, Kennan Papers.

[33]George F. Kennan, "Comments on the National Security Problem," March 28, 1947, Kennan Papers.

[34]Kennan to George C. Marshall, March 15, 1948, *FRUS/1948*, III, pp. 848-849; *Memoirs: 1925-1950*, p. 486.

[35]"The International Situation," *supra*, footnote 12.

[36]"Foreign Aid in the Framework of National Policy," *supra*, footnote 6.

[37]Kennan, *supra*, footnote 26, p. 270 (emphasis added). For a less explicit expression of what appears to be the same thought, see George F. Kennan, *American Diplomacy 1900-1950*, Chicago: University of Chicago Press, 1951, pp. 5-6.

[38]Kennan, *supra*, footnote 10, p. 582.

[39]*Ibid.*, p. 581.

[40]*Ibid.*, p. 575 and pp. 581-582.

[41]"Russia's National Objectives," *supra*, footnote 17. See also the transcript of the discussion following this lecture.

[42]"Russia's International Position at the Close of the War with Germany," in Kennan, *Memoirs: 1925-1950*, p. 535.

[43]Unsent letter to Walter Lippmann, April 6, 1948, Kennan Papers.

Biographical Sketch
of George F. Kennan

George Frost Kennan, currently professor emeritus of historical studies at the Institute for Advanced Studies at Princeton, was born in February 1904 in Milwaukee, Wisconsin, and entered the Foreign Service of the United States in 1927. He served at Hamburg, Tallinn, Riga and Berlin before being reassigned to Riga as Russian language officer in 1931. Because of his command of the Russian language, he accompanied Ambassador William C. Bullitt to Moscow to reopen the American Embassy in 1933. He served in Moscow again from 1935 to 1938, then in Prague, then again in Berlin; became counselor of legation in Lisbon, in 1942; was a member of the U.S. delegation to the European Advisory Commission, London, in 1944; and was assigned as minister-counselor in Moscow 1945.

After a year as faculty advisor at the National War College, Kennan became director of the State Department's Policy Planning Staff in 1947, and Counselor of the Department in 1949. He was a member of the Institute for Advanced Studies, Princeton University, 1950-52, was appointed Ambassador to the Soviet Union 1952, and retired from the Foreign Service in 1953, when he again became a member of the Institute for Advanced Studies. Recalled to active service, he was Ambassador to Yugoslavia 1961-63. Returning to Princeton, he became professor and served until 1974, when he became emeritus.

Among his books are two that won the Pulitzer Prize: *Russia Leaves the War* (1956) and *Memoirs 1925-1950* (1967). Other important works include *American Diplomacy 1900-1950; Realities of American Foreign Policy; Soviet-American Relations 1917-1956; Russia, the Atom, and the West; Russia and the West Under Lenin and Stalin; On Dealing with the Communist World; Memoirs 1950-1963;* and his most recent book, *The Cloud of Danger*, published in 1977.